ISO 2.
GUIDANCE ON PROJECT MANAGEMENT
A POCKET GUIDE

Other publications by Van Haren Publishing

Van Haren Publishing (VHP) specializes in titles on Best Practices, methods and standards within four domains:
- IT and IT Management
- Architecture (Enterprise and IT)
- Business management and
- Project management

Van Haren Publishing offers a wide collection of whitepapers, templates, free e-books, trainer materials etc. in the **Van Haren Publishing Knowledge Base**: www.vanharen.net for more details.

Van Haren Publishing is also publishing on behalf of leading organizations and companies: ASLBiSL Foundation, CA, Centre Henri Tudor, Gaming Works, IACCM, IAOP, IPMA-NL, ITSqc, NAF, Ngi, PMI-NL, PON, The Open Group, The SOX Institute.

Topics are (per domain):

IT and IT Management	Architecture (Enterprise and IT)	Project, Program and Risk Management
ABC of ICT	ArchiMate®	A4-Projectmanagement
ASL®	GEA®	ICB / NCB
CATS CM®	Novius Architectuur Methode	ISO 21500
CMMI®	TOGAF®	MINCE®
CoBIT		M_o_R®
e-CF	**Business Management**	MSP™
Frameworx	BiSL®	P3O®
ISO 17799	EFQM	PMBOK® Guide
ISO 27001/27002	eSCM	PRINCE2®
ISO 27002	IACCM	
ISO/IEC 20000	ISA-95	
ISPL	ISO 9000/9001	
IT Service CMM	OPBOK	
ITIL®	SAP	
MOF	SixSigma	
MSF	SOX	
SABSA	SqEME®	

ISO 21500
Guidance on project management

A POCKET GUIDE

Anton Zandhuis, PMP
Rommert Stellingwerf, MSc, PMP

Van Haren
PUBLISHING

Colophon

Title:	ISO21500: Guidance on project management – A Pocket Guide
Series:	Best Practice
Authors:	Anton Zandhuis, PMP
	Rommert Stellingwerf, MSc, PMP
Reviewers:	Ben Bolland (BEVON Gilde)
	Stanisław Gasik (Vistula University)
	Martin Rother (QRP)
Text editor:	Steve Newton
Publisher:	Van Haren Publishing, Zaltbommel, www.vanharen.net
ISBN hard copy:	978 90 8753 809 5
ISBN eBook:	978 90 8753 770 8
Print:	First edition, first impression, May 2013
Layout and type setting:	CO2 Premedia, Amersfoort – NL
Copyright:	© Van Haren Publishing, 2013

In this publication illustrations and texts have been reused with permission from British Standards Institute (BSI):
'Permission to reproduce extracts from BS ISO 21500:2012 is granted by BSI. British Standards can be obtained in pdf or hard copy formats from the BSI online shop: www.bsigroup.com/Shop or by contacting BSI Customer Services for hardcopies only: Tel: +44 (0)20 8996 9001, Email: cservices@bsigroup.com'

© 2012 BSI for Figure 2.1; Table 2.1; Annex B Glossary

For any further enquiries about Van Haren Publishing, please send an e-mail to: info@vanharen.net
Although this publication has been composed with most care, neither Authors nor Editor nor Publisher can accept any liability for damage caused by possible errors and/or incompleteness in this publication.

Preface

Project management is one of the key skill sets demanded by organizations around the world. Some facts:

- One-fifth of the world's GDP, or more than $12 trillion, will be spent on projects each year in the decade 2010-2020[1].
- In the coming years many skilled project management practitioners will be leaving the workforce due to retirement — a trend which will have a major strategic impact for over 60% of the organizations worldwide[2].

Consequently there is a great demand for knowledgeable project managers.

The intention of this pocket guide is to provide you with a quick introduction to one of the latest developments in the project management profession: ISO 21500 'Guidance on project management' being the *first really globally accepted standard on project management*. This guide contains a brief and straightforward introduction and high level summary of ISO 21500, with tips for its practical application. It is therefore key knowledge for a project manager who is ready for the future.

It will enable and support you, your organization and all project stakeholders to speak 'one language' in project environments, even cross-borders, with multiple nationalities and multiple organizations involved. It will explain ISO 21500, its background and its practical application.

In 2006 ISO recognized the organizational need for knowledgeable project managers and decided that organizations could benefit from some guidance in this area. An international team of over one hundred experts in project management worked for five years to develop a globally accepted guideline on project management. This development didn't start from scratch; instead it integrated the knowledge from reputable representatives in the project management profession from all over the world, like PMI and IPMA. All this work resulted in a rather slim document. However the impact of ISO 21500 on the project management profession is huge. Committing to ISO 21500 means that all of the stakeholders in project environments speak the same language and work with the same 'big picture' in mind, thus improving communication. ISO 21500 is, therefore, a fundamental input when cooperating in projects and jointly striving for project success.

With ISO 21500 being the first guidance on project management that is accepted and recognized by most of the international organizations which represent and contribute to the project management profession, it will become the *key reference* for future developments in this profession. This fact is already confirmed by e.g. the latest (fifth) edition of PMI's PMBOK Guide (2013), which shares exactly the same structure with only slightly different names for some processes, and which overlaps with more than 95% of the processes mentioned in ISO 21500. Other globally applied standards, like IPMA's Competency Baseline 4.0 (due in Autumn 2014), already plan to follow the same direction.

Is it important for you to know? Well, nowadays every organization has projects, whether formally recognized as such or not. Projects are mostly aimed at achieving new organizational capabilities, for meeting new demands, driven by the increased pace of change in the organization's environment, or for realizing new opportunities. So it is more than likely that at some point in time during your professional career you will have a role to play in these projects. For that reason it is important for you to have some basic understanding of project management. No matter what your role in the project is, project manager, project sponsor, project team member: all stakeholders speaking the same language in projects is key to facilitating communication, and increasing the speed, quality and chances of project delivery.

We would also like to underline that all these projects represent large investments by organizations, as we have mentioned in the beginning. But moreover, think about the time and effort spent by scarce resources. For organizations it has become essential to deliver their projects successfully to ensure a sustainable future. That takes more than a skilled, experienced, knowledgeable and competent project manager. It requires basic project management knowledge from all project stakeholders and some well-defined processes, applied in practice, to facilitate real cooperation and ensure realizing the drive to make it happen. If this teamwork is based on a (well) defined, shared and well understood approach, it will increase the success rate of projects, delivering or even exceeding the expected benefits.

We encourage you, your project management community and project stakeholders collectively, to become familiar with ISO 21500, its concepts, subject groups (themes) and its processes, in order to increase successful project delivery!

May 2013,

Anton Zandhuis
Rommert Stellingwerf

Acknowledgements

The authors wish to thank Van Haren Publishing for their vision and the opportunity to write and publish this pocket guide.

We are grateful for the cooperation of BSI and their permission to use parts of the BS ISO 21500:2012 document.

We have been inspired by some of the analysis work of the 'ISO 21500 interest group' especially for chapter 7, where we compare ISO 21500 with other standards and methods. This interest group was initially formed in 2009 to review the usability of the forthcoming ISO 21500 guideline in the Netherlands, and is sponsored by IPMA-NL and PMI Netherlands Chapter. Given the enthusiasm of its members for the development of the project management profession, and the open discussions and sharing of ideas and insights, it is now continuing as 'ISO for projects' in order to further contribute to the promotion and practical implementation of the ISO 21500 guideline, as well as to assess the application of the new ISO documents for program and portfolio management and for project governance, which are all under development at the time of writing.

We also appreciate that the reviewers spent time to read our manuscript and forward their comments to us. We have incorporated their valuable input where applicable in the final manuscript.

And last but not least, we would like to thank our partners and children for not complaining when we could not share quality time with them because of our commitment to the planning and the writing of this book.

Table of contents

1 Introduction

1.1 Purpose of this pocket guide to ISO 21500

ISO 21500 provides **generic guidance on the concepts and processes of project management** that are important for the successful realization of projects. This pocket guide is intended as a brief reference to assist in quickly understanding the purpose, background and key elements.

What is the value of ISO 21500? This new globally accepted project management standard is recognized as a foundational reference for the application of project management knowledge and good practices. Research has confirmed that, when managing projects, the structured application of this fundamental knowledge and good practices clearly enhances successful delivery. Project environments that consistently apply this fundamental project management good practice approach not only show better project performance in terms of lower costs and shorter delivery times, but they also demonstrate higher levels of customer satisfaction. The application of the project management good practices, as described in ISO 21500, will support you in realizing these benefits.

In addition to the above, when working in a project management environment, for which the organization is far more dynamic than 'normal' operations, there is an increased need for good communication. To achieve this, it is important to use 'one common language' within your project management environment, which is understood by everyone involved, particularly the key stakeholders of the project. This pocket guide aims to quickly establish a shared vocabulary and terminology on the project management fundamentals and create a common understanding about the basic project management processes together with the key roles and responsibilities. Moreover the guide provides a high level description of how the ISO 21500 guideline can be applied in practice, using a 'generic' project life cycle as a reference.

What it's not? It is definitely not 'the' solution for all challenges when managing projects. The project manager and the team remain ultimately responsible for deciding what good practices shall be applied to the specific project at hand, in close cooperation with the project sponsor and the management of the line organization or sponsoring entity.

In a nutshell, this pocket guide is intended as a key contributor and tangible asset when introducing and reinforcing concepts of project management in your organization for improved communication and cooperation. It supports an organization-wide implementation of a project management culture, bringing you the benefits of 'your projects executed right the first time'! At the organizational level this can be enhanced by implementing a project management approach, based on these good practices.

1.2   Practical tips for using this pocket guide

On the fold out at the back cover of this book, all subject areas and applicable processes and chapter numbers are listed. Key project management terms and definitions are explained in the Glossary of the ISO 21500 terminology, in Appendix B.

1.3   Why apply project management?

Every organization has its unique culture and faces diverse challenges. Also, organizations start with a different situation and set of problems to be resolved. In order to define the value of project management, we firstly need to define exactly what is meant by project management, as this is a broad concept. Then we can look at the various aspects of project management and show the value associated with each aspect.

> *Project management – ISO 21500 definition:*
> Project management is the application of methods, tools, techniques and competences to a project. Project management includes the integration of the various phases of the project life cycle. Project management is accomplished through processes.

Research shows that, with the increasing complexity and faster changing environments that businesses are faced with, projects managed by the structured application of good practice-based processes show consistently better performance in areas such as, but not limited to:

- 'Deliver as promised' by realistic expectation-setting through up-front project definition, planning, and estimation;
- Faster delivery through the reuse of common and known project management processes;
- Less 'surprises' during project execution, utilizing proactive project management processes;
- Improved customer satisfaction and less rework by delivering the right product or service, right, the first time.

These opportunities together with the savings offered by organizational project management excellence are all tangible. But the value proposition for project management is much greater and also includes less tangible benefits like:

- A highly committed and motivated team that can work together through effective communication and goal setting;

- An inspiring project environment with a 'can-do' mentality through ambitious yet realistic commitments;
- Transparent and improved decision-making at all organizational levels through more effective communication.

These qualitative benefits will even reinforce the quantitative advantages, which will guarantee that an organization is able to excel.

Many organizations have built a good reputation for being able to consistently deliver top quality projects. However, a majority of organizations are still struggling with this. Do you recognize the following characteristics?

- Projects mostly deliver late, over-budget, or without meeting the functionality requirements of the project sponsor and end-users;
- Project managers do it 'their way' as there are no, or poor, standards for project management processes and techniques;
- Project management is regarded as an overhead instead of being recognized as providing business value;
- The project work undertaken by resources from within the line organization is not carefully planned for as part of the operations planning, but is typically regarded as 'next to your primary function';
- Project budgets do not include the cost of the internal workforce as they are 'already paid for';
- There is no overall insight available on all the projects being undertaken in the organization, nor their cost versus the added value;

- The required work for managing projects proactively is not included in the project plan;
- Projects may be somehow 'successful' in the end but only through heavy stress and overtime work.

> *Do you recognize the above in your project environments? Having more disciplined project management is the way to overcome these shortcomings. The value of a good project management practice, using common project management processes, will enable better communication to deal with contingencies pro-actively. This will substantially and continuously increase the chances of project success. It will establish new management procedures and processes. It will enable you to run your organization as an economic enterprise.*

1.4 Successfully fulfilling your role as project sponsor, project manager or project team member

Understanding your role in a project and acting accordingly is vital for project success. Therefore we highlight the three key roles which are the major contributors in realizing a successful project:

1 The **project sponsor** acts as the continuous link between the funding organization(s) and the project. It is the sponsor who is responsible at the start for defining the Business case for the project; why should we be doing this project; what are the organization's needs? When the project is approved, the project manager takes over the responsibility for 'delivery

of the defined project objective'. The sponsor still fulfills
an ever- important role for ensuring the project objective
is aligned to the project goal. The sponsor should, amongst
other things, ensure that the organization sticks to its initial
decisions regarding goal setting, thus preventing constant
priority changes based on daily operational issues. The project
sponsor, therefore, plays an important role in ensuring that
there is sufficient support from functional and operational
management, which in turn fulfills a key role in assigning the
appropriate resources to the project team. The sponsor should
also support the organization's readiness to effectively deal
with the project objective when it is delivered, as this is where
the benefits realization, and consequently increased business
value, will start. In order to achieve this, the project sponsor
must work closely together with the project manager. The
fluent communication between these two roles is crucial for
both the project and organizational success.

2   The **project manager** is ultimately responsible for the delivery
    of the defined project objective. Key elements in this role are
    stakeholder management, and guiding the project team and
    the appropriate stakeholders in selecting and applying the
    right project management processes at the right time. But
    everything must be undertaken with an eye on the delivery
    of the project objective. The project manager must take
    advantage of the project sponsor's business knowledge and
    influential position, and escalate all issues or business- related
    problems that cannot be solved by the project management
    team.

3   The **project (management) team member** is typically
    responsible for delivering the expertise and work needed

to create the project result. During the initial phases of the project, their focus is on defining the best approach and developing a feasible high-level plan for the project; in other words, the planning. During the execution phases, based on their expertise, they realize the project objective and specific subcomponents. It is essential to ensure that the organization which takes over the responsibilities at the end of the project is adequately represented within the project team. This will facilitate a smoother transition of the project objective to the operational or sponsoring organization.

In every project these key roles that are needed for the successful delivery of the project should be clearly described and understood, so that all stakeholders can act accordingly.

Figure 1.1 clearly describes the common relationships between the sponsor organization/entity and the project organization, and shows where each role is positioned.

Note: The sponsor organization/entity should be interpreted in the widest sense to cater for the differences in the various environments in which projects are undertaken.

Projects can run in one single organization, such as one company, business or governmental department. In that case the project results (or deliverables) are normally accepted by Operations in the line organization. However, projects can also be executed by more than one organization (e.g. a joint venture) or in the case of large investment projects they can act more or less independently, like a temporary organization (e.g. for the construction of a railway). In the latter cases we do not have a single sponsor organization, but a sponsor entity, that eventually accepts the

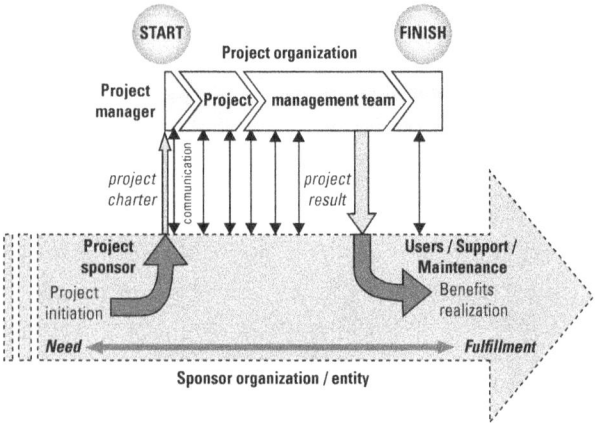

Figure 1.1 Common relationships between sponsor organization/entity and project organization

project results. Clearly the project governance is also more complex in the latter cases.

1.5 Frequently asked questions

We have identified some typical questions that one could ask when first confronted with project management or the ISO 21500 guideline.

What is a project?

> *Project – ISO 21500 definition:*
> A project is a unique set of processes consisting of
> coordinated and controlled activities with start and finish
> dates, undertaken to achieve an objective. Achievement of
> the project objective requires deliverables conforming to
> specific requirements, including multiple constraints such as
> time, cost and resources.

- This means: It has a defined start and finish, therefore a
  project is temporary;
- 'Something' is finished when the project is finished; it creates
  an end deliverable, the project objective;
- It is not business as usual, and as a consequence does not
  follow normal procedures, because there is something unique
  to it;
- Given the above, it needs a specific organization for the
  coordination and control of this unique set of processes.

Although within an organization some projects may be similar,
each project is actually unique as differences may occur e.g.
in the deliverables provided by the project, the stakeholders
influencing the project, the resources used, the way processes
are adapted to create the deliverables, etc.. Because there
are projects of all types and levels of complexity, the project
management activities and the underlying processes should
be geared to the project at hand. But it's the organization's
responsibility to firstly decide if the desired objective should be
realized through undertaking a project. If that is the case, then
the project should be organized accordingly.

Is 'project management' a profession?

While there is no agreed definition of a 'profession', you could describe it as:

'A disciplined group of individuals who adhere to defined ethical standards and uphold themselves to the public as having specific knowledge and skills in a generally recognized, organized body of learning, derived from education and training, and who apply this knowledge and these skills in the interest of others.'

With projects getting more and more complex, the demands on a project manager's competence are also increasing. For example, everyone can apply a bandage to a wound but that does not make everyone a doctor. The need to obtain specific skills, knowledge and education, in order to successfully fulfill the role of project manager, is generally recognized. This is even confirmed in the academic world where Masters degrees in project management are now available.

Characteristics of a professional discipline also include the use of a common vocabulary. The ISO 21500 terms and definitions provide a foundational professional vocabulary of specific project management terms, in addition to commonly used terminology, which is already defined in the Oxford Dictionary.

Given the fact that, due to the ISO processes being followed for the creation and global acceptance of the content of ISO 21500, apparently there is consensus about what can be regarded as a set of foundational:

- Terms and definitions;
- Concepts, including competences;
- Processes.

ISO 21500 also states that successful management of projects requires people who are competent in project management principles and processes. ISO 21500 defines, but does not limit, at least three categories of project management competences which are needed in order to apply project management:

- Technical competences, for delivering projects through applying the project management processes in a structured way;
- Behavioral competences which refer to the capabilities required to build and reinforce relationships, beneficial to the project, within the organizational environment;
- Contextual competences, which relate to adjusting the project management processes to the organizational environment.

One can, therefore, safely conclude that 'project management' has matured into a profession.

Can you manage a line organization (operations) effectively without projects?

Line organizations are typically function-centric and, in general, focus on ongoing day-to-day operations, while 'doing their thing better'. Operations can therefore become resistant to (major) changes, particularly when the driver for such a change lies outside their own functional responsibilities and needs.

Projects and project management, on the other hand, are all about implementing necessary changes in operations, in order to stay in business. The realization of the project's objective and its application in operations might even threaten the effectiveness and efficiency of specific operational entities (e.g. departments, business units), but is nevertheless executed to enable whole organization to perform more effectively.

And the reality is that hardly any organization can survive in today's environment without having projects. At times they are not formally recognized but organizations undertake them anyway. The increasing number of 'reorganizations' reflect this, with a constant drive for ensuring that the line organization keeps up with the increasingly complex and ever-faster changes in the environment. The increasing number and scope of changes, as well as the risks associated with these, are demanding greater focus and attention on projects, together with the need for a more professional approach towards project management. This is because this type of professional approach ensures that the changes are delivered and managed in an appropriate way. It will support line organizations in continuing to 'do the right thing, the best way' and getting ahead.

What is the purpose of ISO 21500?
ISO 21500 describes a professional approach towards project management, which is applicable to most projects, most of the time. It is, therefore, very likely that your projects can benefit from it. This approach is based on its proven value and benefits in practice, through the contribution of hundreds of experts in the project management profession, from all over the world, who base their expertise on the experiences of thousands of project practitioners worldwide in conjunction with in-depth studies. Making this knowledge available to a wider audience, in a well structured and easy to understand way has been the key-driver for developing this standard; for the aim is improved communication and cooperation in projects environments, thus increasing project success.

Is ISO 21500 a method or methodology?

ISO 21500 is referred to as an informative standard; a guideline.
A guideline can be defined as a basic conceptual structure to
allow homogeneous handling of different business processes
grouped together. It also increases management discipline. It
pre-defines common deliverables to and from each business
process. A guideline provides a model with a well-defined tactic
to master the complex environment of an organization in a simple
fashion. It acts as a taxonomy or map of the entire body of project
management knowledge.

A method is defined as a particular procedure for accomplishing
or approaching something, especially a systematic or established
one[3]. A method not only mentions the process, but also describes
how a task is completed; a more detailed prescribed way to
execute the processes.

A methodology is defined as a system of methods used in a
particular area of study or activity[4].

Being a basic reference ISO 21500 is a guideline rather than
a method or methodology. Although the common project
management processes are described (the 'what'), they do not
prescribe the exact way of doing (the 'how'). In practice, for the
implementation of this guideline, several project management
methods and methodologies can be defined and applied, and then
fine-tuned towards the application area and specific subject of the
projects. But before one can select, define, or apply any project
management method or methodology, there should first be a
thorough and common understanding of the project management
terms and definitions, concepts and processes.

What if you want to know more about ISO 21500?

Creating a shared view, a common structure, and then consistently building on that, is essential for clear and concise communication. For this reason we have simply maintained the well-considered structure of ISO 21500 as defined in table 2.1. When looking for a more detailed explanation and understanding about a certain process, we simply refer to the related chapter and section number in ISO 21500.

Can you get certified on ISO 21500 as an organization?

Certification, also known as third party conformity assessment, is the provision by an independent body of written assurance (a certificate) that the product, service or system in question meets specific requirements. Many companies and organizations decide to get certified to one of ISO's management system standards, such as ISO 9001 as a way of showing outsiders that the organization has an effective quality management system in place.

As ISO 21500 is an organizational standard, with currently the status of a guideline or 'informative standard' one cannot obtain an ISO certification (like with ISO 9001). It is expected that over time, when the market shows an interest, the guideline can be upgraded to a 'normative standard'. In that case organizations can be certified by nationally acknowledged accreditation bodies. In the meantime, however, organizations can perform a 'self-assessment' (see section 2.7 and Annex A).

Can you get certified on ISO 21500 as an individual?

Because ISO 21500 as 'informative standard' now, or 'normative standard' in the future, is aiming at organizations and not at individuals, individual certification is not possible.

However there is a globally recognized individual certification track, organized by PMI, using A Guide to the Project Management Body of Knowledge (*PMBOK® Guide*) as a reference. There is huge similarity in the structure and content of ISO 21500 and the PMBOK Guide:

- The 10 Subject groups in ISO 21500, are equal but called knowledge areas in the PMBOK Guide;
- 39 project management processes in ISO 21500 versus 47 in the PMBOK Guide, however only with slightly different naming and some processes further detailed in the PMBOK Guide, thus leading to a higher number.

PMI uses the PMBOK Guide (and therefore essentially ISO 21500) as a basis for its globally recognized individual Project Management certifications for the typical project manager roles: Certified Associate in Project Management (CAPM) and the Project Management Professional (PMP). Based on the above, one can safely conclude that a PMI certified project manager (PMP) not only understands the ISO 21500 concepts, but is able to apply these in practice as well. PMI does not issue organizational certifications in the same way as ISO or ANSI, however PMI does offer Organization Project Management Maturity Model (OPM3) as an assessment method for organizations.

Also IPMA maintains an individual certification track, which uses the three competence areas as a reference (further detailed in chapter 5). Within these three areas more detailed competences are defined, including possible process steps. Most of these competences clearly relate to the ten Subject groups as defined in ISO 21500. Other competences are more related to methodologies which are not part of ISO 21500. IPMA also

does not issue organizational certifications in the same way as
ISO or ANSI. However IPMA is developing IPMA Delta as a
project management assessment for the entire organization, due
Autumn 2013.

How can ISO 21500 support you in real-life application?

As ISO 21500 is based on globally recognized and accepted
good practices, it can effectively act as a 'foundational worldwide
lessons learned database' for project management. Based on its
structure and well defined processes, it will definitely turn the
mind-set in organizations from an 'ad-hoc' and fire-fighting mode
(reactive management), which is still too often experienced in
projects, towards a more proactively oriented and well organized
approach (project management). It enables you, your project
team and project stakeholders, when faced with challenging
project situations, to proactively refer to the appropriate project
management processes and fine-tune these to your project.
It directly enhances project communications by creating a
common understanding of 'projects', 'a shared vision on how to
best manage these', resulting in a shared project management
approach for successful team work.

How does ISO 21500 align with other methods, practices and models?

ISO 21500 provides a guideline that is generally accepted
as global good practice for project management. Therefore
it is a perfect guideline for creating and understanding your
organizational project management approach, which needs
to fit with your specific projects in your specific environment.
This is typically where the project management processes
and the content creation processes should be integrated.

'Drowning' people in several different approaches, with different backgrounds and definitions and having each individual doing their own 'integration exercise', is likely to cause confusion, errors and miscommunication, as well as being inefficient. A well-organized comparison of the processes, terms and definitions of ISO 21500 with the processes, terms and definitions of other methods, practices and models applied in your organization, will enable a quick identification of any potential overlap, and enable effective integration in an appropriate way. In Chapter 7 we provide additional insights into how ISO 21500 compares to other commonly used project management methods, practices and models.

How does ISO 21500 address the different organizational entities and levels?

Organizations develop procedures for delivering results in a predictable way that allow them to manage expectations. However, as most projects are cross-functional, several organizational entities typically come together in projects and are required to deal with situations not encountered before, and for which no procedures are defined (as yet). When projects result in changes in organizations, different stakeholders are involved at different organizational levels, i.e. operations level, tactical level, and even strategic level. Therefore the understanding and application of a common organization-wide reference for managing projects, such as ISO 21500, is of particular value in such situations. In separate sections of the concepts in Clause 3, ISO 21500 addresses 'Organizational strategy and projects', 'the Project environment', 'Project governance' and 'Projects' and 'Operations' as well as how these can interact.

Is ISO 21500 likely to supersede your current (perhaps organizationally developed) project management method or practice?

Organizationally developed project management methods and practices typically stem from a recognized need for improvement in the application of project management, based on organizational experiences and good practices. As ISO 21500 is also quite often based on the same, practices, the majority of your own project management method will not drastically change. However, maintaining your own developed good practices, as well as ensuring continuous alignment with the latest developments in the project management profession and possible changes in your environment, or internal processes can become very costly and time consuming. This could be a key driver for organizations to switch to ISO 21500 as their basic reference for a project management method or practice and only adjust this where necessary for their specific projects and environments, and document these changes or additions transparently. Following the Pareto rule; around 80% of the guideline is likely to be generally applicable to your type of projects. This allows a focus on the specific 20% of the project management processes that form the uniqueness of your specific organization and project environment. This then becomes the heart of your own project management method or practice.

The generic publicly available project management methods, practices and models are now starting to point to ISO 21500 as a basic reference (PMI's PMBOK Guide – Fifth Edition, January 2013; IPMA's ICB version 4.0, due Autumn 2014; IPMA Delta - project management assessment for the entire organization -, due Autumn 2013; The GPM Reference Guide to Sustainability in Project Management[5], January 2013). In such cases the knowledge contained in ISO 21500 substantially supports the better understanding and positioning of these project management methods, practices and models, thus reinforcing the correct application.

What if I need more information?

As this is a pocket guide, it should be viewed as an introduction to and summary of ISO 21500. Many more details and explanations on certain topics can be found on the ISO website, or more specifically in the document ISO 21500:2012 Guidance on project management, or the national version of this.

2 ISO 21500 background and overview

This chapter describes the ISO organization, the development process of its standards and the background, benefits, structure and future of the ISO 21500 document.

2.1 ISO organization

ISO (International Organization for Standardization) is the world's largest developer of voluntary international standards. It was founded in 1947 and since then has published over 19,000 international standards, which give state of the art specifications for products, services and good practice, helping to make industry more efficient and effective. ISO is a network of national standards bodies in 164 countries, which make up the ISO membership and represent ISO in their country.

ISO mission:
- 'The mission of ISO is to promote the development of standardization and related activities in the world with a view to facilitating the international exchange of goods and services, and to developing cooperation in the spheres of intellectual, scientific, technological and economic activity.'

ISO objectives:
- 'Conformity assessment': checking that products, materials, services, systems, processes or people measure up to the specifications of a relevant standard or specification. Today, many products require testing for conformity

with specifications or compliance with safety, or other regulations before they can be put on many markets. ISO guides and standards for conformity assessment represent an international consensus on best practice. Their use contributes to the consistency of conformity assessment worldwide and so facilitates trade.
- 'Certification': ISO does not carry out accreditation or certification to any of its standards; there exist many testing laboratories and certification bodies which offer independent conformity assessment services.

2.2   ISO standards development process

Via the national standards bodies, subject matter experts from all over the world participate in the standards development through a global, open and transparent process aimed at achieving consensus. The forming of a shared view on the contents of a standard is a long process, but this means in the end that the ISO standards are widely supported.

The development process is organized via:
- Project or technical committees, which formulate the scope of the standards and organize meetings with international experts to discuss and write the contents of the standards and process the received comments;
- National mirror committees, which appoint subject matter experts to take part in the development and comment on the draft standards.

On average, developing an international standard takes approximately four years.

2.3   ISO standard versus guideline

ISO develops international standards. A standard is a voluntary
agreement between stakeholders on a product, service, result
or process. The agreements contain terms and definitions,
functional and performance related requirements, processes,
measuring methods and good practices.

Two kinds of standards exist:
- Of *descriptive* (informative) nature;
- Of *prescriptive* (normative) nature.

If one talks about a *standard* one normally means the prescriptive
standard. A descriptive standard is often called a *guideline*.
A guideline presents the course of action with regard to the
demands of goods, services and people. A guideline does not
specifically describe what to do, that is the goal of a prescriptive
standard. Prescriptive standards are often the next logical
step, after descriptive standards have been implemented in
organizations and have globally been accepted as a good practice.

2.4   Background of ISO 21500

This section discusses the economic driver for developing
ISO 21500, along with the process and the sources which have
been used for its creation.

The economic driver to develop ISO 21500

One-fifth of the world's GDP, or more than $12 trillion, will
be spent on projects each year in the next decade[1]. This is an
enormous investment, which calls for prudent spending and
proper management control.

Since the industrial revolution, standardization has been an important prerequisite for growth. Recent research indicates that today's businesses face economic pressure from clients and other stakeholders to meet their needs faster and more cheaply than ever[6].

In today's world, investments and organizational changes are realized via projects and programs of related projects. For many of these projects a variety of disciplines and a mix of internal and external workers are involved. All these people need to cooperate in a proper way, everyone has to carry out his/her tasks effectively and, at the same time, all this work must be aligned and executed in a process-driven way. A great number of project management methods and practices exist. Who can apply these properly? Which method should be chosen in a multidisciplinary project? How does one communicate with the stakeholders? These questions do not have easy answers.

In the past there have been a number of initiatives aimed at developing global project management standards, like Global Project Management Forum (from 1994), PMBOK Guide (ANSI standard, First Edition in 1996), Operational Level Coordination Initiative (OLCI, from 1999), Global Alliance for Project Performance Standards (GAPPS, from 2002) and ISO 10006 – Quality management systems – Guidelines for quality management in projects, 2003). They all failed to produce one body of project management knowledge that was accepted globally. ISO 21500 – Guidance for project management is the step towards the true world standard for project management.

The development process of ISO 21500

In 2006 the United Kingdom submitted a proposal to develop a new international standard for project management, which later became known as ISO 21500. With the forthcoming 2012 Olympic Games in London they realized that their current standard developed by the BSI (British Standards Institution) needed a revision. The United States supported this proposal and it went for ballot to the 164 countries that have an ISO representation. A majority of ISO members voted positively and the ISO/PC (Project Committee) 236 was established at a meeting in October 2007 in London with the charter to develop the standard.

Hundreds of project management experts and their mirror committees from more than 30 countries have co-operated during the five years of its completion. The participants have discussed the contents, wrote the body text and processed more than 1,000 comments that came up per draft version. An international project team that worked very well together came into being, because the same 80 – 100 delegates participated in the various international meetings.

The large project management associations were involved in various ways. PMI (Project Management Institute) was the secretary of ISO/PC 236. IPMA (International Project Management Association) formally took part in the development in a liaison role. There was no noticeable representation of UK's Cabinet Office (owner of PRINCE2). Of course, a number of experts in the working group were also members of these associations or holders of their professional certifications and have represented the associations' views via their involvements.

The sources for ISO 21500 development

ISO 21500 has a broad target audience that uses various sources for project management. Therefore, the support for the guideline – first by its developers and later by its users – had to be the core of project management that is relevant for everybody. All country mirror committees had the opportunity to bring in relevant sources of project management as input for the guideline at the start of its development in 2007. They proposed the following national standards:

1   A Guide to the Project Management Body of Knowledge (*PMBOK® Guide*)-Third Edition, Chapter 3 and Glossary, PMI Inc., 2004 – the American ANSI standard;

2   DIN 69901 Project Management: Project Management Systems, DIN, 2007 – the German DIN standard;

3   BS 6079 and BS ISO 15188:2001 – Project management, BSI, 2001 – the English BSI standard.

In the course of the ISO 21500 development other market standards and existing ISO standards have been used as reference materials:

1   ICB version 3.0 (IPMA Competence Baseline) – by International Project Management Association;

2   PRINCE2 (PRojects IN Controlled Environments) – by Cabinet Office, previously OGC;

3   ISO 9001 – Quality management systems;

4   ISO 10006 – Quality management systems – Guidelines for quality management in projects;

5   ISO 31000 – Risk management – Principles and guidelines.

The benefits of ISO 21500

The ISO 21500 guideline is not a new project management standard, but a reference for other project management standards, methods and best practices, such as PMBOK, PRINCE2, Agile and ICB. It does not compare one against the other, but brings the best project management practices together.

The importance of ISO 21500 is that it introduces one global standard and language for the project management practice. It is overarching and a reference point for all projects in all organizations.

One can use the ISO 21500 guideline as follows:

- *As a reference in an audit*
  If an organization's project management practice complies with the requirements and criteria of ISO 21500, it has a good foundation for competent project managers to achieve proper project results. At the same time, the organization can prove both internally and externally that it delivers quality projects, because they have based it on the independent standard. Indeed, this guideline does have direct influence on the *project execution*, but not on the *project result* as such;

- *As a link between different project management and business processes*
  ISO 21500 can supplement the ISO 9001 for quality management, especially in the area of continuous improvement: realizing the necessary and wanted improvement processes in operations with minimal disturbance of the production and service processes;

- *As a checklist to prove the knowledge and skills of project managers and project workers in executing projects*
  The guideline looks at one project at a time. It does not refer to more complex situations, like multi-project management

or sub-projects. This makes the guideline accessible for a broad target group, who can simply relate their own role to the guideline. ISO 21500 strongly emphasizes the role that the environment plays during the execution of the project in order to maximize the added value of the deliverables of the project;

- *As a common reference (bridge function) between different methods, practices and models*
  Existing project management methods like PRINCE2, collections of good practices like the PMBOK Guide, and competence models like ICB 3.0, provide an anchor to the project manager when running a project. A concise and clear guideline will attract parties that are not familiar with these existing methods, practices and models;

- *As a common language in project management*
  ISO 21500 bridges the differences and reinforces the similarities between the many parties that often work together in a project: sponsor, project manager and his colleagues, project organization, project workers, customers, users and/or the internal organization. ISO 21500 supports the communication between the related parties by offering a common language. A common language is also essential with international and/or multi-disciplinary projects, where different teams work with different methods, and where cooperation is necessary. The guideline can then be a binding factor by relating the processes and deliverables of the different methods to those of ISO 21500.

2.5 The contents of ISO 21500

This section highlights the scope and the structure of the ISO 21500 contents.

The scope of ISO 21500

The scope of ISO 21500 is to provide guidance for project management and may be used by any type of organization and for any type of project.

The guideline provides a high-level description of concepts and processes that are considered to form good practice in project management.

Projects are defined in the context of programs and project portfolios. Guidance on their management will be the subject of separate ISO standards.

The structure of ISO 21500

The guideline is structured as follows:
- Clause 1 Scope;
- Clause 2 Terms and definitions;
- Clause 3 Project management concepts;
- Clause 4 Project management processes;
- Annex A (Informative) Process group processes mapped to subject groups.

Clause 1 covers the scope of ISO 21500, i.e. the management of projects in 'most organizations most of the time'.

Clause 2 contains 16 project management terms and their definitions. It contains only those specific terms that from a project management practice viewpoint are not properly defined in the standard lists of ISO definitions or in the Oxford English Dictionary. The glossary in Annex B of this pocket guide presents this list of terms and definitions.

Clause 3 describes the concepts which play an important role during the execution of most projects:

- Project;
- Project management;
- Organizational strategy and projects;
- Project environment;
- Project governance;
- Projects and operations;
- Stakeholders and project organization;
- Competences of project personnel;
- Project life cycle;
- Project constraints;
- Relationship between project management concepts and processes.

These concepts and their relationships are shown in figure 2.1.

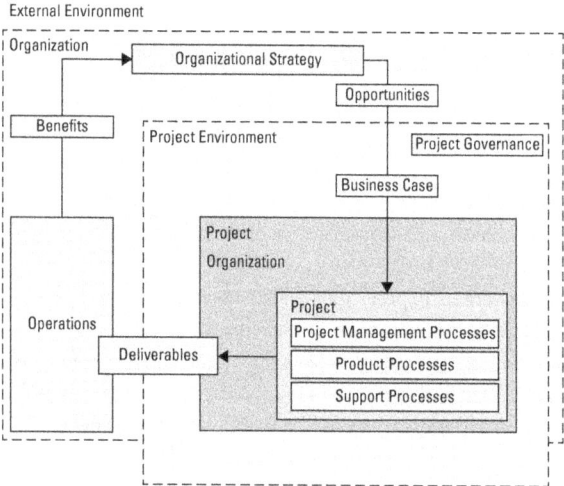

Figure 2.1 Project management concepts in organizations and other sponsor entities[7]

In fact these concepts are centered around *value creation* in an organization (e.g. an internal investment in a business or a (non-) governmental organization) or a sponsor entity (e.g. a railway owned by a governmental entity). The organizational or entity strategy creates opportunities which are evaluated and selected, for example in a *portfolio management* process. Business cases for selected opportunities may result in one of more projects with deliverables. These deliverables are normally used by operations to realize benefits and thus create value for the organization. The benefits can be input to realize and further develop the strategy. In commercial projects the benefits are realized without passing deliverables to operations.

Clause 4 identifies the recommended project management processes that should be applied to the whole project and/or to project phases. These processes are generic and can be used by any project in any organization or entity. Normally, the project manager and the sponsor select the applicable processes and the sequence in which they are dealt with, depending on the project at hand and the needs of the organization or entity.

The project management processes are viewed from two different perspectives: as *process groups* from the management perspective of a project, or as *subject groups* from the perspective of a specific theme (refer to the *knowledge areas* in PMI's *PMBOK Guide*) of the project management practice.

There are five *process groups*:

1 Initiating;
2 Planning;
3 Implementing;
4 Controlling;
5 Closing.

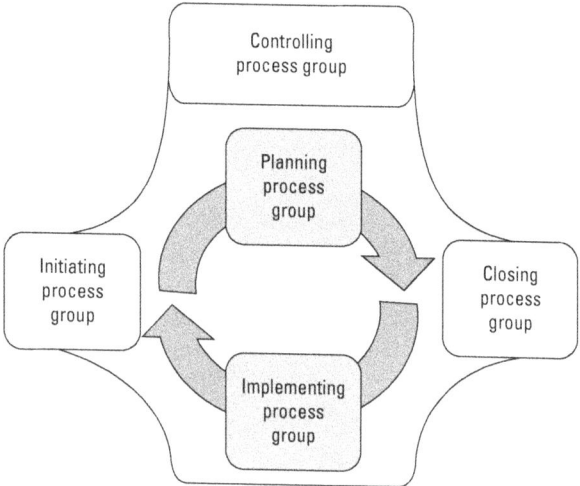

Figure 2.2 Process groups[7]

These process groups are based on the well known Deming
Circle (Plan-Do-Check-Act) for continuous improvement.

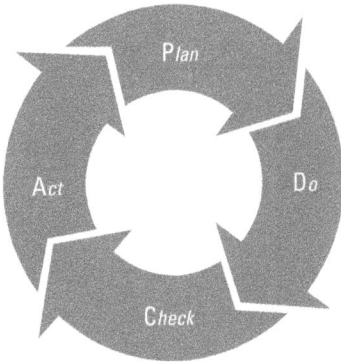

Figure 2.3 Deming Circle

There are 39 *processes*, divided into ten project management
themes, called *subject groups*:

1 Integration;   6 Cost;
2 Stakeholders;   7 Risk;
3 Scope;   8 Quality;
4 Resource;   9 Procurement;
5 Time;   10 Communication.

The processes are summarized by process and subject groups in
Table 2.1.

The table does not show the chronological order in which the
processes are carried out.

Table 2.1 Overview of the project management processes[7]

Subject groups	Process groups				
	Initiating	Planning	Implementing	Controlling	Closing
Integration	4.3.2 Develop project charter	4.3.3 Develop project plans	4.3.4 Direct project work	4.3.5 Control project work 4.3.6 Control changes	4.3.7 Close project phase or project 4.3.8 Collect lessons learned
Stakeholder	4.3.9 Identify stakeholders		4.3.10 Manage stakeholders		
Scope		4.3.11 Define scope 4.3.12 Create work breakdown structure 4.3.13 Define activities		4.3.14 Control scope	
Resource	4.3.15 Establish project team	4.3.16 Estimate resources 4.3.17 Define project organization	4.3.18 Develop project team	4.3.19 Control resources 4.3.20 Manage project team	

Subject groups	Process groups				
	Initiating	Planning	Implementing	Controlling	Closing
Time		4.3.21 Sequence activities 4.3.22 Estimate activity durations 4.3.23 Develop schedule		4.3.24 Control schedule	
Cost		4.3.25 Estimate costs 4.3.26 Develop budget		4.3.27 Control costs	
Risk		4.3.28 Identify risks 4.3.29 Assess risks	4.3.30 Treat risks	4.3.31 Control risks	
Quality		4.3.32 Plan quality	4.3.33 Perform quality assurance	4.3.34 Perform quality control	
Procurement		4.3.35 Plan procurements	4.3.36 Select suppliers	4.3.37 Administer procurements	
Communication		4.3.38 Plan communications	4.3.39 Distribute information	4.3.40 Manage communications	

Within the processes all activities are performed that are relevant for managing a certain aspect in a project. All of the processes transfer inputs into useful outputs, which can, in turn, be inputs to other processes. Typical inputs/outputs here are project management documents, such as a project plan, a schedule, a contract, or a progress report. Only the most relevant inputs/ outputs are listed in ISO 21500.

In **Annex A** of the original ISO 21500 an example of a possible logical sequence of the processes is included for a particular project.

2.6   The future of ISO 21500

ISO 21500 has been written as a guideline and because it does not contain requirements, it is in principle not meant for certification purposes. This differs from, for instance, the normative standard ISO 9001 'Quality management systems', which describes management systems for an organization to manage and improve its processes or a certain aspect of its operations. An organization can make the effort to become ISO 9001 certified to improve its quality and service to customers and clearly display its performance to the business environment.

As for every ISO standard and guideline, it is likely that ISO 21500:2012 will be updated in the next four to five years to integrate new developments and new best practices for project management. This next version could have a normative nature and then certification of organizations might be possible.

As an intermediate step towards organizational certification, a so called 'self-assessment' could be developed. To this extend, the developments which happened for the ISO 21600:2010 may

Figure 2.4 ISO 26000 Guidance on social responsibility

serve as an example. To support and promote the interest for ISO 26000:2010 – Guidance on social responsibility a 'Self-assessment ISO 26000' has been developed[8, 9, 10].

This self-assessment is not a certification but is a declaration of how an organization applies the principles and guidelines of ISO 26000. By publishing these self-assessments in a central database, organizations can prove that they operate sustainably and in a socially responsible way.

A similar self-assessment could be beneficial to organizations that run projects. Nowadays tenders for project work often prescribe that the supplier uses a specific project management method. One can foresee that in the near future project sponsors will require their suppliers to show that their project management practice conforms to ISO 21500.

Annex A of this pocket guide presents an example of what a 'ISO 21500 self-assessment' could look like. At the time of writing this book, there is an initiative in the Netherlands to develop such a self-assessment for the Dutch market.

3 ISO 21500 and roles and responsibilities

This chapter provides a definition of the roles and responsibilities and categorizes the stakeholders who can be identified in a project. It then describes typical roles of people working in the project organization, the PMO and the project management consultancy organization. Finally it describes some specific roles in very large (complex) projects and when projects face governmental constraints.

3.1 Roles, responsibilities, tasks and activities

Role and responsibilities of each stakeholder should be clearly defined and communicated during the course of the project. From this it should be evident which tasks they have to perform in the project.

A *role* is the function assumed or part played by a person or thing in a particular situation[11]. The project role is the function/title of a person in the project, e.g. project manager, project sponsor, customer.

A *responsibility* is a thing which one is required to do as part of a job, role, or legal obligation[12]. The project responsibilities are the clear description of what each person working in his/her project role should do, including the person's authorities and accountabilities.

A *task* is a piece of work to be done or undertaken[13]. Project tasks include activities to actually create (part of) the project objective (also often called product components or product deliverables) and/or to produce a project document for managing the project, e.g. project charter, project plan, schedule, action list (often called project management products or project management deliverables).

An *activity* is a thing that a person or group does or has done[14]. Project activities are being used to describe the work to be done in a project management process and may include one or more tasks.

3.2   Project stakeholders in ISO 21500

The project stakeholders who are in any way affected by the project are described in ISO 21500 and shown in figure 3.1.

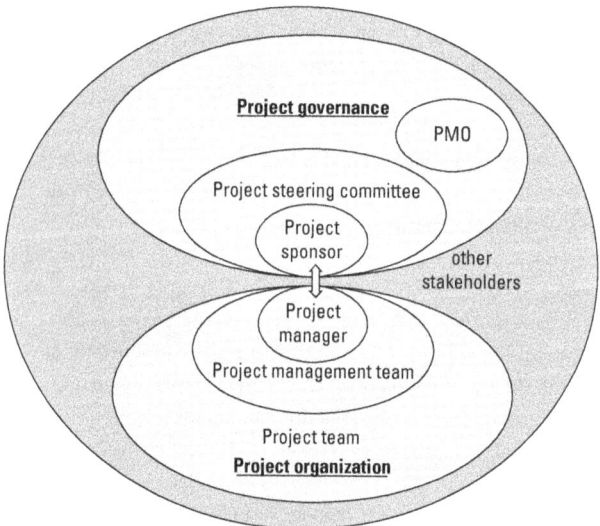

Figure 3.1 Internal and external project stakeholders

The project stakeholders are divided in two groups: those
within the project organization and within project governance are
called the *internal stakeholders* (grey) and the others are called
the *external stakeholders* (blue).

1. Project organization
The *project organization* is the stakeholder group that performs
all of the work to realize the project objective:
- Project manager – the manager of the project and responsible
  for the successful completion of the project;
- Project management team – the people assisting the project
  manager in managing the project;
- Project team – the people who perform project work.

2. Project governance
Project governance is part of the corporate governance that deals
with directing and controlling projects from an organizational
perspective and establishes the proper environment to run
projects. It is the framework and principles through which
projects, programs and project portfolios are authorized and
overseen.

Typically higher management, the sponsor, the project steering
committee and the PMO (project management office) belong to
the project governance group:
- Project sponsor – the representative of the organization that
  owns and funds the project;
- Project steering committee – the senior managers and the
  project manager who together direct the project from the
  perspective of the organizational strategy and the Business
  case (benefits realization);

- PMO – the group that supports the practice of project management and execution.
  Note: In ISO 21500 the PMO is included with the 'other stakeholders', but depending on its role it might also fit in the 'project governance' group, as depicted in figure 3.1.

3. Other stakeholders

The *other stakeholders* are all other individuals and groups who are not part of the project organization nor of project governance, but who are directly or indirectly affected by the execution or the deliverables of the project, for example:

- Customers or customer representatives – the people that define the requirements and receive the deliverables of the project;
- Suppliers (vendors, contractors, third parties) – those that supply human resources, facilities or materials to the project;
- Employees, shareholders, business partners, special interest groups, finance providers, regulatory bodies, etc.

3.3   Benefits of ISO 21500 for some specific roles

In the following paragraphs we describe examples of some specific roles for which knowledge of ISO 21500 can be useful in supporting the application of project management.

Roles in a PMO

In ISO 21500 the PMO (project management office) is one of the stakeholders, see above. The PMO, sometimes called PSO (project support office), can take many shapes in the organization and may perform diverse activities, such as:

- Governance, ensuring how projects are directed and controlled;

- Deciding on project management methods, tools and techniques;
- Training of project management staff;
- Planning and control of one or more projects, or of a collection of projects in a program or portfolio;
- Project audits and reviews.

It could act at a corporate level, as an 'independent' corporate department reporting to the executive management team, or at a lower departmental level e.g. as a team in the section where projects are executed, or it could even be part of the project organization, as is often seen in large projects.

The following roles can be recognized in a PMO:
- Head PMO – the manager of the PMO team;
- Project advisor – the person who (in)directly supports the projects that are being executed, in some way;
- Project controller – the project advisor with the main role to support the project and financial planning and control of projects or collections of projects.

To properly perform these roles some form of standardization of project work is needed; the advisor can use the definitions, concepts and processes of ISO 21500 to shape the project management practice in their own organization. By adopting ISO 21500 the PMO ensures that the organization adheres to a worldwide accepted project management practice, which makes working in or for projects, where many organizations have to work together, more easy.

Roles in a project management consultancy organization

Nowadays there are many organizations that provide project management consultancy, ranging from training in project management methods, tools and techniques, through to advising on projects or sourcing project staff. Such staff can work as either an internal or external contractor on (part of) a project.

The following roles can appear in a project management services organization:
- CEO – the chief executive officer/director of the consultancy organization;
- Account manager – the interface between (new) customers and the project staff on (new) work;
- Project consultant – the person providing consultancy and advice on a specific project;
- Project manager – the manager of a single project;
- Project team member – the person working on a project;
- Trainer – the person providing PM training and individual coaching for their project roles.

ISO 21500 does not focus on this type of organization specifically, but it is very important for them because it is the globally accepted and independent project management practice. The PM consultancy organization can generate new business by developing training for ISO 21500, gaining expertise in ISO 21500 in order to assist other businesses in applying the new guideline and aligning the execution of their projects to ISO 21500.

Roles in a complex project

In general, a complex project will be large in size and duration, require huge funding, carry high risk and deal with many (external) stakeholders, because it often affects the general public. Examples are: the building of a refinery, the construction of a railway, or the organization of the Olympic Games.

For such a complex project the project organization and the personnel aspects normally require special attention, as it is the essential foundation for its future success. It is essential that sufficient human resources, including other critical resources, are available to carry out all the work to complete the project. It must be ensured that the different project team roles and the responsibilities are described properly, based upon which resources with the right skill sets are assigned to the project. For complex projects, it is also essential to identify the key (external) stakeholders and manage their expectations properly, as these external stakeholders can sometimes 'make or break' the project.

And for complex projects it is critical to establish the project governance correctly. Inadequate governance is one of the main reasons that complex projects often do not run satisfactorily. The temporary project organization runs almost autonomously. There should be a strong alignment to corporate governance in order to ensure and maintain proper support from the project environment. This aspect is difficult and therefore needs specific attention.

To function properly the definition and assignment of the governance roles need special attention and ISO 21500 gives a good indication of what roles are required here. The complex project should have:
- An active sponsor – who has a direct link to the project manager to express commitment for project success from both sides and to promptly deal with issues of any kind;

- A project steering committee – of senior managers from both the client and the contractor organization sides to monitor and control the project;
- Its own PMO (project management office) – to support the project directly.

Because complex projects are often public (infrastructure) projects, the whole project organization should demonstrate ethical and responsible conduct for the benefit of the society and the environment.

So, the bottom line challenge here is that, in practice, many different parties will have to communicate effectively in order to work together successfully, whilst recognizing that all stakeholders have their specific interests and roles, as well as using their own cultures (national as well as organizational), procedures and project management practices as a basic reference. To improve the communication between all stakeholders ISO 21500 can act as an effective common reference for managing a complex project.

Roles in a project with governmental constraints
Projects with governmental constraints (more on constraints in chapter 4) require special attention. These constraints could be procurement-related (e.g. using an international tendering process), fixed yearly budgets (e.g. for large infrastructure projects requiring public funds), legal obligations (e.g. the implementation of the Sarbanes-Oxley Act of 2002 – new or enhanced standards for all U.S. public company boards, management and public accounting firms – or the implementation of Basel III – a global, voluntary regulatory standard on bank capital adequacy, stress testing and market liquidity risk in

response to the deficiencies in financial regulations revealed by the late-2000s financial crisis), public/private projects (e.g. a new highway), and so on.

ISO 21500 can well be applied to projects in governmental settings which have to deal with these special constraints. The focus here will be on managing the interests of their specific stakeholders, relating to:

- Public responsibility;
- Sensitivity for fraud;
- Broad internal and external support;
- Risk management, focusing on security and reliability;
- Proper use of public resources.

A number of specific roles, beyond those mentioned in ISO 21500, are required to properly deal with governmental constraints in a project:

- Sponsor – representative of the government that launches the project, provides the funds and becomes the 'owner' of the deliverables at the end to ensure that the benefits are achieved, which makes the government spending defendable;
- Contractors – firms that actually carry out the work and realize the project objective;
- Project steering committee – consisting of senior managers of both government and contractor, ensuring that the project is delivered successfully within the given constraints;
- Project manager – needs to have experience with these governmental assignments, given the special constraints which need to be managed;
- Governmental experts – individuals with the appropriate knowledge of confederational or federal regulations

    (European Union, United States), national, or local
    government;
- Internal and external auditors – ensuring compliance with
  organizational and legal constraints;
- General public – often the user of the end product of an
  infrastructure project (e.g. a new train line).

For projects which have to deal with governmental constraints as
described above, paying sufficient attention to managing specific
stakeholders by attracting specialist roles such as those above to
the project will significantly increase their chance of success. For
specialists, given their different backgrounds and experience,
ISO 21500 can act as a common reference for managing such
projects.

4 ISO 21500 and balancing the project constraints

4.1 Constraints and their importance

What is a constraint?

The Oxford English Dictionary defines a constraint as:
a limitation or restriction[15].

In the Theory of Constraints[16], developed by Eliyahu Goldratt, a constraint is defined as anything that limits a system (which can be project) in reaching its goal. This is a very broad definition, because it encompasses a wide variety of possible constraining elements. Constraints could be physical (equipment, facilities, material, people), or they could be policies (laws, regulations, or the way we choose to do business—or choose not to do business). Frequently, policies cause physical constraints to appear.

Why is it important to understand the project constraints?

While the project manager and the team try to realize the project's objective, based on the requirements for the project, the project will be faced with different constraints. Constraints can, therefore, be regarded as a specific subset of requirements, with a limiting or restricting character. It is important for a project manager to balance these constraints, as constraints are often interrelated such that a change in one may affect one or more of the others. Hence, the constraints may have an impact on the decisions made within the project management processes. If the constraints are too limiting and impossible to balance, it may become impossible for the project to realize its objectives within the stated requirements.

A well reasoned and maintained agreement on the constraints between the key project stakeholders forms a strong foundation for project success.

4.2   Typical constraints

There are many different constraints that may be imposed on a project. The typical constraints often mentioned in project management concepts are: Scope, Time and Cost (also referred to as the Triple Constraint, Project Management Triangle or the Iron Triangle) where each side represents a constraint.

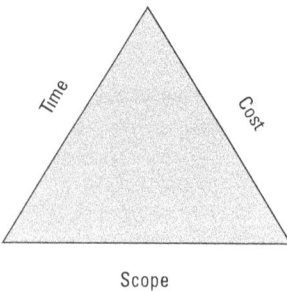

Figure 4.1 Triple Constraint

- The constraint of Time refers to the amount of time available to complete the project (the 'deadline');
- The constraint of Cost refers to the financial limitations based on the funding available for the project;
- The constraint of Scope refers to 'all the work' that must be done to produce the project's end result for meeting their requirements.

A further refinement of the constraints integrates Quality and Scope in 'Performance' (= scope at a certain quality) or turns Quality into a fourth constraint. Other project management methods, practices and models go even further by adding, for example, Risks or Resources as additional constraints. The basis nevertheless always goes back to the Triple Constraint.

With a dilemma (choice between two options) already being difficult to deal with, a 'trilemma' is an even more difficult choice given the three options, each of which appears unfavorable. There are two logically equivalent ways in which to express a trilemma: it can be expressed as a choice among three unfavorable options, one of which must be chosen, or as a choice among three favorable options, only two of which are possible at the same time. A third approach, and in projects the realistic way of dealing with this trilemma, is to carefully balance all of the constraints in such a way that the outcome is acceptable to all stakeholders.

This balancing of constraints starts when defining the project, in order to create a realistic and feasible plan that is acceptable to all key stakeholders:

- Increased scope mostly leads to increased time and increased cost. Although end-users of course would like to get the 'perfect' solution, it's still the sponsor who has to provide the funding for that;
- A very tight deadline, which could be demanded by the sponsor, but could lead to increased costs and reduced scope, which may not be acceptable to end-users as it might create unfavorable working conditions since the end solution is far from perfect;

- A very tight budget which could lead to reduced scope, and once again may not always be acceptable to end-users or other stakeholders.

So, one side of the triangle cannot be changed without affecting the others. And speaking of change: when executing the project, changes will definitely happen. The project manager then has to constantly manage and rebalance the constraints in order to respect all stakeholder requirements sufficiently. Frequent communication with key stakeholders about their constraints is therefore essential. It's the discipline of project management that enables the project team (not just the project manager) to organize their work in such a way that it will meet all constraints, thus satisfying the stakeholders' requirements, including any limiting requirements.

On top of the previously mentioned 'Triple Constraint', ISO 21500 also mentions other constraints like:
- Limited availability of project resources such as people, facilities, equipment, materials, tools and others required;
- Safety constraints;
- Risk limiting factors;
- Ecological impact;
- Laws, rules and other legislative requirements.

But other constraints to take into account might be:
- Specific parties to work with (partners);
- External dependencies;
- Durability of the solution;
- etc.

It's the project management team's job to define and document the constraints and manage these during the project life cycle. Given the 'source' of most constraints there is a strong relationship between:

- The impacting constraints and their relative importance (which constraint takes priority when faced with a dilemma?);
- And the project environment and the key-stakeholders (what is their level of 'power').

The chances of success for the project management team significantly increase if this relationship is managed properly.

Identifying and managing constraints becomes a little easier if there is an orderly way of classifying them. A suggested way of categorizing constraints is using the following seven basic types[15]):

- *Market: limited demand for a product or service.* In most project environments this typically relates to the project Business case and therefore it's the main responsibility of the project sponsor. Increased collaboration between project manager and sponsor can significantly improve the Business case and therefore can reduce the limiting effects of constraints e.g. funding limitations.
- *Resources: not enough people, equipment, or facilities to satisfy the demand for products or services in time.* In most project environments resources are obtained from the line organization. A stronger and more compelling Business case, and clear communication about the effects of decisions in the line organization for ensuring sufficient resource availability may change the willingness of the organization to actually provide the right resources in time.

- *Material: inability to obtain required materials in the quantity or quality needed to satisfy the demand for products or services.* In most project environments materials are either acquired from the line organization or via suppliers/vendors (see below). For internally acquired materials, as with resources, a stronger and more compelling Business case, or clear communication about the expected effects of decisions ensuring materials availability may change the willingness of the organization to provide the right materials (sufficient and of the right quality) in time.

- *Supplier/vendor: unreliability (inconsistency) of a supplier or vendor, or excessive lead time in responding to orders.* In most project environments materials are either acquired from the line organization (see above) or via suppliers/vendors. For externally acquired materials, a more strict selection of procurement parties may prevent supplier/vendor constraints, or a different type of contract (incentives) may lead to a different way of cooperation between the buyer and the vendor (partnership), thus limiting the effects, or even removing these constraints completely.

- *Financial: insufficient cash flow to finance the project.* For externally funded projects, payment could be planned and aligned to the cost plan (budget) or to the work items completed. For internally funded projects, the scope of the first project could be reduced to the lowest level of objective, which is confidently expected to achieve the initial benefits (savings, revenues, other financial benefits). Optimization of benefits realization (program management) enables the program to become financially self-sustainable.

- *Knowledge/competence: necessary information or knowledge is not available within the project team or people don't have the skills (or skill levels) necessary to deliver the required*

project objective. Typically a team composition issue which
can be resolved by either sourcing the critical knowledge or
competences (usually with cost consequences) or training the
available team members (usually with a time consequence).

- *Policy: laws, regulations, internal policies and procedures or
  business practices that inhibit progress toward the project's
  objective.* Laws and regulations require interpretation. By
  thoroughly studying the laws and regulations, this often leads
  to identifying opportunities that were previously unknown.

Internal policies and procedures, next to being very supportive
and preventing that the project has to 'invent everything', may
also act as major constraints. These policies and procedures
are typically created for the optimal functioning of a line
organization. At some level, these processes can become quite
large and complex, such as a production process, a purchasing
process, or a marketing and sales process. One way of dealing
with complexity is to compartmentalize it, by creating functional
departments. Each department is responsible for some function
that constitutes a part of the whole system. Procedures and
policies are then created in an orderly way to deal with the
issue of complexity in a predictable, cost efficient manner.
Efficiency and effectiveness are key – but focused on their 'own'
departmental objective!

Projects are typically cross-departmental, and for good reasons!
A project is defined and a project manager assigned, because the
line organization is not capable (as it doesn't have the appropriate
structure for it) of creating that specific and unique objective,
as required by the project sponsor. Projects therefore quite
often need to have some own policies and procedures, which

are defined to optimally facilitate the creation of the project's objective.

In cases where a project has to comply with all of the policies and procedures defined by each department involved in the project, it may be just as well not to create a project with a project manager with some level of authority. For such an initiative, it could be better to assign an 'expediter' instead, who has no authority but simply follows and 'facilitates where possible' every cross-departmental step of the objective's components in the complete chain of production and implementation. In reality the key-driving constraint simply remains the efficiency and effectiveness of the individual departments. The creation of the specific objective is automatically treated as of secondary importance, which of course needs to be recognized and accepted by the sponsor of the initiative (expectation management) since organizational constraints 'always' take priority over project constraints.

5 ISO 21500 and competences of project personnel

5.1 Competence

Competence is the ability to do something successfully or efficiently; also competency[17]. While ISO 21500 mentions both competence and competencies, in this book we use competence only.

5.2 Competences of project personnel

ISO 21500 is rather limited on the competences, but nevertheless, in the context section 3.9 of ISO 21500, the competences of the members of the project team are mentioned as a prerequisite to successfully deliver projects. ISO 21500 categorizes these competences in three areas as follows:

- Technical competences;
- Behavioral competences;
- Contextual competences.

It is clear that by mentioning these competences, reference is made to the IPMA Competence Baseline (ICB) version 3.0[18], where these competence areas are described in much more detail.

In the ICB version 3.0 project management is broken down into 46 competence elements, covering three competence areas in the 'eye of competence, see figure 5.1, which represents the

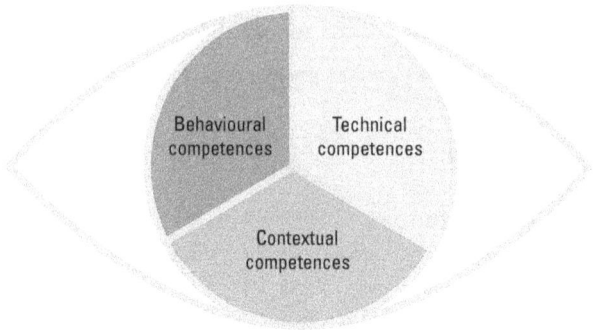

Figure 5.1 The competence eye of the project manager

integration of all the elements of project management as seen by
the project manager, when managing the project:

- *Technical competences* (20) – the hard skills of project
  management, including the project management terminology,
  concepts and processes as they are also described in ISO
  21500;

  1. Project management
     success
  2. Interested parties
  3. Project requirements
     and objectives
  4. Risk & opportuntity
  5. Quality
  6. Project organisation
  7. Teamwork
  8. Problem resolution
  9. Project structures
  10. Scope & deliverables

  11. Time & project phases
  12. Resources
  13. Cost & finance
  14. Procurement & contract
  15. Changes
  16. Control & reports
  17. Information &
      documentation
  18. Communication
  19. Start-up
  20. Close-out

- *Behavioral competences* (15) – the soft skills of the project personnel, their professional behavior within the boundaries of the project; essential to bring projects to a successful conclusion;

1. Leadership	8. Results orientation
2. Engagement & motivation	9. Efficiency
	10. Consultation
3. Self control	11. Negotiation
4. Assertiveness	12. Conflict & crisis
5. Relaxation	13. Reliability
6. Openness	14. Values appreciation
7. Creativity	15. Ethics

- *Contextual competences* (11) – the skills related to properly understanding the project environment, including project governance and the way programs and portfolios are managed. Understanding and properly applying these skills is an important aspect for everyone working on a project.
    1. Project orientation
    2. Programme orientation
    3. Portfolio orientation
    4. Project, programme & portfolio implementation
    5. Permanent Organisation
    6. Business
    7. Systems, products & technology
    8. Personnel management
    9. Health, security, safety & environment
    10. Finance
    11. Legal

The project management competences of all project personnel should be known and, if necessary, they should develop these

via training, coaching and mentoring for their individual
development, or for the needs of a particular project.

Also see section 7.3 for a comparison between ISO 21500 and
ICB 3.0

6 ISO 21500 Subject groups

ISO 21500 recognizes two perspectives for structuring the project management processes, either by Process group (Initiating, Planning, Implementing, Controlling and Closing) or Subject group. A Subject group is a project management theme. This chapter describes the Subject group perspective in order to provide a better understanding of the contents of ISO 21500.

ISO 21500 contains ten Subject groups in total. Every Subject group collects the processes by subject and each process is shown in the Subject group in which most of its related activities are performed.

6.1 Integration Subject group

The Integration Subject group is about planning the work and working the plan. It covers the start and finish of the project and everything in between. It is about finding balances between competing constraints and requirements, finding alternatives and handling the dependencies between the various project management Subject groups.

Like the spider in the web, the Integration Subject group coordinates and integrates the processes from all the other Subject groups.

There are seven Integration Subject group processes in total:
1 *Develop project charter:* the process to document the high level requirements and project boundaries – the charter will authorize the project manager to start the project or phase;

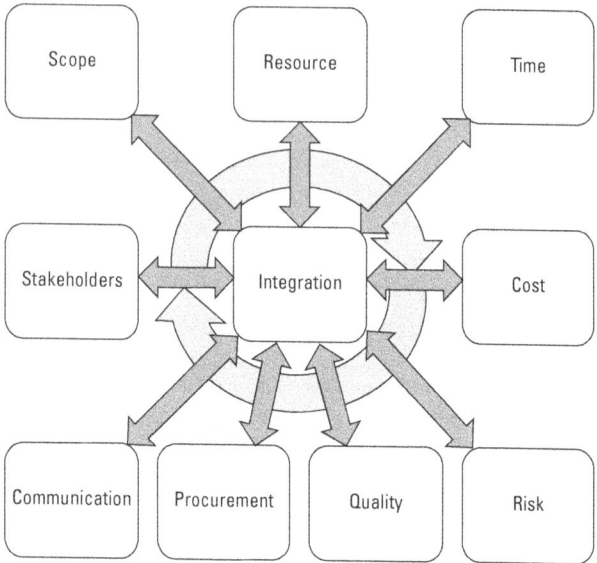

Figure 6.1 The process scheme of Integration Subject group

2　*Develop project plans:* 'plan the work'; compiling the overall
  plan by capturing the subsidiary plans that originate from the
  other nine Subject groups. Typically two plans are mentioned:
  the Project management plan (describing how the project will
  be organized and controlled) and the Project plan (an outputs-
  based description, starting high-level and progressively
  elaborated throughout the life cycle of the project, defining
  the baselines for scope, cost, time, etc., which will be updated
  throughout the project);

3　*Direct project work:* 'work the plan'; direct the team members'
  activities required to create the project deliverables;

4 *Control project work:* this is managing the project's progress and performance compared to the plan and the initiation of process changes in order to improve performance;

5 *Control changes:* a process for structuring the way in which the project deals with change requests and how changes are managed to the plan (formal acceptance or rejection) and to the deliverables;

6 *Close project phase or project:* completing all activities to close a phase or the project including the formal verification and acceptance of completed project deliverables;

7 *Collect lessons learned:* generating and documenting key positive and negative performances during the project to act as useful references for planning future project phases or other projects, thus increasing the organization's project management maturity (increasing effectiveness and efficiency in project performances).

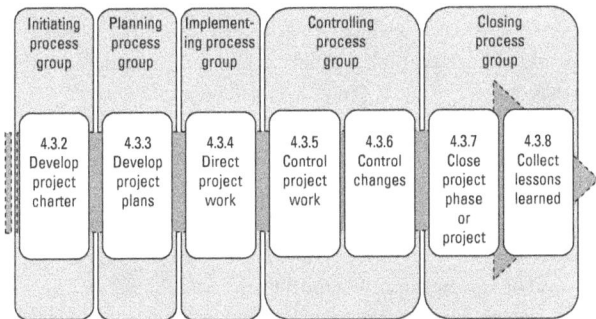

Figure 6.2 Overview of Integration Subject group processes

6.2   Stakeholder Subject group

This subject group includes all of the steps necessary to identify the people, groups, or organizations that could impact, or

be impacted by, the project. We try to analyze stakeholder
expectations and their impact on the project. We try to analyze
stakeholder impact on the project and their associated needs. We
try to develop appropriate management strategies for effectively
engaging and communicating with stakeholders during the
project duration.

Stakeholder satisfaction should be managed as a key project
management objective.

Stakeholders are part of every project and they can be impacted
by, or can impact, the project in a favorable or less favorable way.
Some have a limited ability to influence the course of the project,
while others have more influence on the project and its outputs.

The Stakeholder Subject group has two processes:
1 *Identify stakeholders:* understanding the stakeholder
   environment is a key input for scope definition. By
   overlooking a key-stakeholder you may well miss 100% of
   their requirements. If you've ever had the experience of being
   forced to 'squeeze' requirements into a project which was
   perceived as 'nearly finished', you will not be surprised by
   the fact that you may have to rework a significant part of the
   project scope, with devastating consequences for both time
   and cost (triple constraint!), quite apart from the expected
   level of acceptance and support by that stakeholder, whose
   'existence' you have forgotten....
2 *Manage stakeholders:* making sure that stakeholders with a
   positive interest are behaving positively towards your project
   (don't lose your friends; you might need them ...!) and that
   stakeholders with a negative interest are unable to destroy

your project (keep your friends close, watch your enemies even closer). By taking a proactive look at your project from their perspective you may be able to predict 80% of their expected behavior, and organize accordingly in advance. If you don't manage your stakeholders they will manage you, resulting in reactive management, instead of project management!

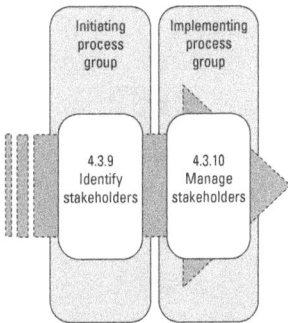

Figure 6.3 Overview of Stakeholder Subject group processes

6.3 Scope Subject group

The Project Scope is the answer to the 'what' question: what 'product' will the project deliver and what intermediate results need to be produced to get the 'end product'. This includes the product scope, the features and functions characterizing the project end-result, as well as the project scope, all the work required to deliver the aforementioned product scope.

The Scope Subject group covers all processes required to define and control the work that is needed (in scope) and not needed (out of scope) to deliver the project result.

The processes in the Scope Subject group are:

1 *Define scope:* creating a Scope statement including the link to the organizational strategy, defining and documenting stakeholders' needs to meet the project objectives and creating a description of the project boundaries and its product (project end state);

2 *Create work breakdown structure (WBS):* breaking down project deliverables and project work into smaller and more manageable components;

3 *Define activities:* defining an overview of the tasks required to create the detailed or 'operational' project plan for implementing, controlling and closing components of the WBS;

4 *Control scope:* monitoring the status of the project scope and controlling changes (maximizing positive and minimizing negative) to the Scope baseline.

The Scope baseline consists of the Scope statement and the WBS and its dictionary. This Scope baseline is then monitored, verified, and controlled throughout the life cycle of the project (see figure 6.4).

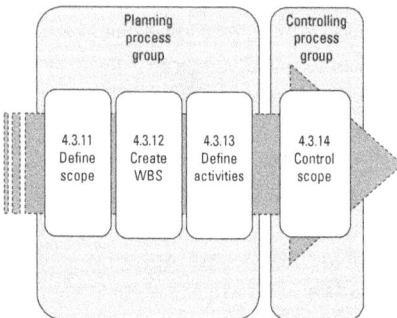

Figure 6.4 Overview of Scope Subject group processes

6.4   Resource Subject group

The Resource Subject group is about getting people on board the project and retaining, leading and managing them, together with obtaining the materials, facilities, infrastructure, etc. The people are called 'project staff' or 'the project team'. It is considered quite beneficial to have the project team assigned and available as early as possible – as their expertise will be used during the planning process and the overall commitment of the team towards the project will be strengthened.

The number of team members might change throughout the course of the project; it depends on the tasks and the work to be done. While the staff are needed for their particular content-related expertise within the project, the project manager's expertise lies in orchestrating their roles and responsibilities, and influencing the project team in terms of communication, politics and organizational issues. In addition, staff may be added to the team for specific project management support, such as scheduling expertise, risk management expertise, or administrative support.

It is necessary to distinguish between the project team and the project management team. The latter is usually a subset of the project team, being concerned with typical project management activities. The project team is the sum of all people working for the project. There might be a programmer assigned 100% to a strategic IT project. If he or she is not involved in project management leadership activities, the programmer is not considered to be part of the project management team but is part of the project team.

The Resource Subject group contains six processes:

1 *Establish project team:* obtaining the resources necessary to establish the project team;

2 *Estimate resources:* determine the resources needed for the project, including human resources, materials, facilities, equipment, infrastructure and tools;

3 *Define project organization:* identifying all team members and other persons directly involved in the project work and obtaining their commitment. Also the definition of roles, responsibilities and authorities that are relevant to the project, aligned with the project's nature and complexity and respecting the performing organization's existing policies.

4 *Develop project team*: establishing the project's ground rules of preferred and acceptable behavior and continuously improving the team performance, interaction and motivation, while respecting and growing the available competences in the project team.

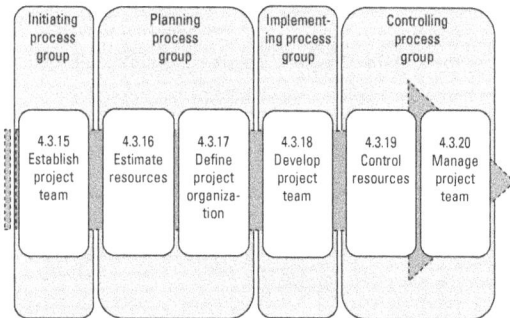

Figure 6.5 Overview of Resource Subject group processes

5 *Control resources:* ensuring that the resources required to undertake the project work are available and assigned to the project, as well as establishing procedures to identify resource shortages, and dealing with conflicts in availability of resources and facilitating their reallocation if needed.

6 *Manage project team:* optimizing team performance, providing feedback, resolving resource issues, encouraging communication, and coordinating changes to realize the project objective.

6.5 Time Subject group

The Time Subject group is concerned with all of the necessary steps to manage the timely completion of the project. Time management seeks to determine feasible delivery dates, milestones or end dates, taking all known constraints into account. Time management is sometimes seen as the core discipline of project management and various popular software tools are available which primarily focus on the time management aspects. The printouts of these software packages are often called the 'project plan'. According to the Time Subject group this is a 'project schedule' and not a 'project plan'.

The Time Subject group covers four processes:

1 *Sequence activities:* identifying and documenting the logical relationships between project activities, providing a network diagram and identifying the critical path;

2 *Estimate activity durations:* estimating the elapsed time to complete each activity in the project, including the time needed for administrative processing and approval, as well as making periodic re-estimates and updated forecasting against the baseline;

3   *Develop schedule:* establishing the overall project schedule
    baseline and subsequent schedule updates, based on
    calculating the start and end times of project activities,
    enabling objective measurement of progress;
4   *Control schedule:* monitoring schedule variances by
    determining the current status of the project schedule and
    comparing it to the approved baseline schedule, and taking
    appropriate actions to avoid adverse schedule impacts.

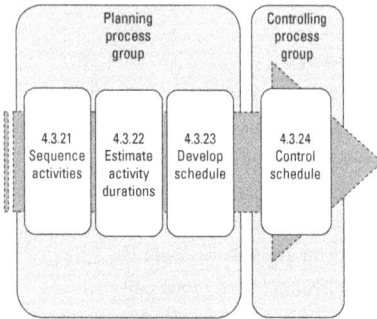

Figure 6.6 Overview of Time Subject group processes

Particularly on projects of a smaller size, the different processes
are so tightly linked that they are often viewed as a single process
that can be performed by one person.

6.6   Cost Subject group

Money is typically one of the key constraints of any project. The
Cost Subject group is therefore all about defining the budget and
managing the actual project cost within the approved budget.
But if the project's primary driver is financial, i.e. approved
investment based on much higher expected savings after project

delivery, it also about safeguarding and possibly improving the financial Business case of the project.

In supplier-customer environments it is necessary to distinguish between the project budget and the potential price of a project (i.e. by selling the result of the project to the marketplace). Project management and especially the Cost subject group are only concerned with the project budget – the price and the respective positive or negative margin of the project deliverables is a management decision outside of the project.

The Cost Subject group contains three processes:

1 *Estimate costs:* estimating the costs needed to complete each project activity and for the project as a whole, including reserves or contingency estimates to deal with risks that have a cost impact;

2 *Develop budget:* distributing the project's budget to the appropriate levels of the WBS;

3 *Control costs:* monitoring cost variances and taking action.

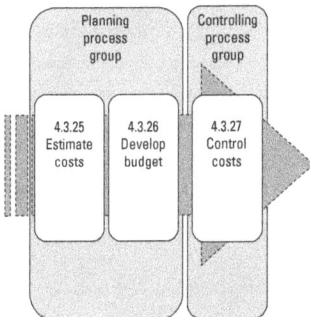

Figure 6.7 Overview of Cost Subject group processes

A project manager needs to be aware of which costs are assigned to the project, how they are assigned and the concept of controlling these costs. In a case where, for example, a project needs a dedicated facility or supporting tool, it is crucial to have a clear view on the mechanics of how costs for this are budgeted. It is also very important to keep an eye on any stakeholder requirements for capturing costs. Different stakeholders may have different views and different requirements on how costs are assigned and reported.

Another aspect of project cost management covers the consequences of project decisions in respect to product maintenance or the cost of product support. E.g. think about the following question: should we keep the project costs low in order to meet the budget, even if the consequence is an expected increase in maintenance costs after the project delivery?

6.7   Risk Subject group

Projects are by definition 'risky' endeavors. It means dealing with unknown situations and as a consequence often resulting in project changes. In order to prevent each project becoming a 'game of chance', the Risk Subject group can support us in controlling the project risks. Project risks are future uncertainties that may affect project results – in both directions, i.e. for the better or worse. Project risks are not business risks, or risks that are related to the performing organization. A project might create such risks, but they are handled from a different perspective.

Risks are uncertainties that matter. It is the job of the project management team to take care of those uncertainties, to identify them, to analyze their impact, to develop responses if applicable, and to monitor and control their effect.

If the project management team neglects risk management, it will be constantly faced with problems on the one hand and missed opportunities on the other. Risk management is about trying to minimize the impact of potential threats on project results, which is usually everything that could cause a project to be delayed, be more expensive, or be delivered with less quality. Risk management on the other hand is also about trying to maximize the impact of potential opportunities; factors which could help to achieve the project results faster, cheaper and with better quality. These need to be actively promoted and supported.

The Risk Subject group has four processes:
1 *Identify risks:* determining potential risk events and their characteristics that, if they occur, may have a positive or negative impact on the project objectives;
2 *Assess risks:* measuring and prioritizing the risks for further action, based on estimating the probability of occurrence of each risk and the corresponding impact on the project objective;
3 *Treat risks:* developing options and determining actions for enhancing opportunities and reducing threats to project objectives;
4 *Control risks:* minimizing disruption to the project in the case of threats, and ensuring maximum optimization of the project objectives in the case of opportunities, by determining whether the risk responses are executed and whether they have the desired effect.

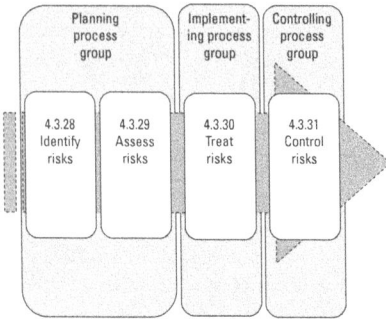

Figure 6.8 Overview of Risk Subject group processes

Risk management processes have little value if they are performed only once, say at the beginning of the project. Constant evaluation is necessary to really harvest the full benefits of risk management.

6.8   Quality Subject group

The Quality Subject group supports the project in achieving its quality objectives.

ISO 21500 recognizes the following three processes in the Quality Subject group:

1 *Plan quality:* gathering all the quality requirements and describing how the project team will demonstrate its quality compliance;
2 *Perform quality assurance:* the process of auditing the quality requirements and application of the quality standards by reviewing the quality control measurements;
3 *Perform quality control:* executing the quality control activities to measure performance and recommend changes if needed.

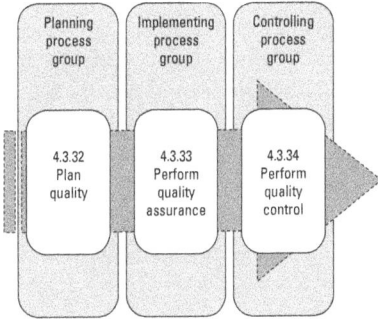

Figure 6.9 Overview of Quality Subject group processes

Failure to meet the project's quality requirements will have a
strong negative impact on project performance and the delivery
of its expected result. This underlines the importance of quality
management. Quality management therefore looks at the
quality of the project product as well as the project management
processes.

Quality can be defined as the level to which a product or service
meets its specification or meets the expectations of its users.
Quality is not synonymous to grade. Grade is an expression of
a product's technical features. Two products or services can
have the same functional use but can have a different number
of features. Where low quality (many defects or not meeting
expectations) is always a problem, a lower grade (less features
and limited functionality) may not be an issue.

Project management and quality management both acknowledge
the importance of customer satisfaction, prevention over
inspection, continuous improvement and management
responsibility for quality. Moreover the Cost of Quality approach

looks even further than simply the project life cycle. The level
of desired quality usually comes with a cost first, because of
the effort needed to achieve it. This is a trade-off that project
management and the sponsoring organization or entity need to
manage carefully because the cost of quality relates to the total
product life cycle and is not limited to the project life cycle only.
Increasing quality as early as possible in the total life cycle will
generally lower the cost. Therefore we emphasize the statement:
Quality is for free!

6.9   Procurement Subject group

As most projects need products, services or resources from
outside the project team, there will be a need to purchase them.
Given the trends of outsourcing to ensure more competitive
cost rates, as well as increasing project complexity which results
in external input being frequently needed by specialists 'not
available in-house', there is an increasing role for suppliers and
partners. One can quickly conclude that a straightforward fixed
price contract is not the best option for every project. When
the contract scope is developed as the project progresses and
the supplier's creativity is needed to get the best result within
a given timeframe, budget or other constraint, more specific
arrangements may be needed.

To deal with these situations effectively, one should apply project
procurement management.

The Procurement Subject group consists of three processes:
1 *Plan procurements:* recording purchasing decisions and
   identifying the approach and the potential suppliers;
2 *Select suppliers:* evaluating the supplier responses, selecting a
   supplier and signing the contract;

3 *Administer procurements:* managing the relationship with the
   supplier, monitoring the supplier's contract performance and
   making adjustments if needed including the completion of the
   contract life cycle for each procured item.

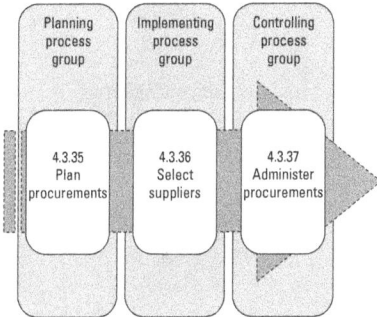

Figure 6.10 Overview of Procurement Subject group processes

Since purchasing a product or a service always implies a legally
binding agreement between buyer and supplier, you are advised
to cover this in a formal contract.

Most organizations will have procurement policies and
procedures that will define the rules to follow if you need to buy
a third party product or service. In many cases you will need to
involve the buying professionals of the organization to make sure
the procurement is done in a professional way consistent with
organizational policies and processes.

The procurement processes actually determine the contract life
cycle. Deciding to buy (a part of) the project result instead of
having it made by the project team could be triggered by a risk
assessment, or a budgetary or time constraint. If, for example,

achieving a part of the project result is considered to be risky, buying that particular piece of work might mitigate the risk.

Every item to be purchased is subject to the three processes outlined previously and to process 4.3.7 Close project phase or project, where the item is actually completed.

Suppliers are also known as contractors, subcontractors, vendors, or service providers. A buyer can be called a client, customer, prime contractor, contractor, acquiring organization, governmental agency, service requestor, or purchaser. The supplier's position during the contract life cycle can change from bidder, via selected source, to contracted supplier.

For the purposes of this chapter we have assumed that the buyer is positioned in the project team and needs to buy items for the project; the supplier is external to the project team. And we have assumed that both buyer and supplier develop a contractual relationship that needs to be managed.

6.10 Communication Subject group

Effective communication enhances the project's chance of success by building stakeholder relationships that can be leveraged to create coalitions and partnerships. It creates bridges between diverse stakeholders involved in a project, and connects various cultural and organizational backgrounds, different levels of expertise, and various perspectives and interests in the project execution or outcome. Project managers spend most of their time communicating or facilitating, and ensuring communication between stakeholders. This starts from day one of the project!

The Communication Subject group defines the key processes
required to ensure timely and appropriate exchange of project
information.

The Communication Subject group has three processes:
1 *Plan communications:* determining the information and
   communication needs of the stakeholders in a communication
   plan;
2 *Distribute information:* making the required information
   available to project stakeholders as defined by the
   communications plan and responding to unexpected, ad-hoc
   requests for information;
3 *Manage communications:* ensuring that the communication
   needs of the project stakeholders are satisfied and resolving
   communication issues if applicable.

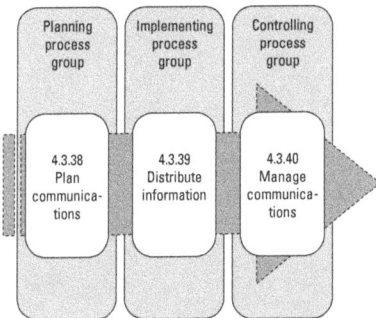

Figure 6.11 Overview of Communication Subject group processes

7 ISO 21500 compared to other methods, practices and models

This chapter compares ISO 21500 with other well known project management methods, practices and models and explains the differences in approach together with the differences and similarities in the project management processes.

7.1 Comparison with the PMBOK Guide

ISO 21500 has been mapped to the PMI's PMBOK Guide-Fifth Edition, issued at the beginning of 2013. The Annex A1 "The standard of project management for a project" of the PMBOK Guide is an ANSI standard. The ISO 21500 processes have been compared with the PMBOK Guide processes. The result is shown in figure 7.1.

The overall conclusion is that:
- ISO 21500 processes have an almost perfect match with PMBOK Guide processes; this is not surprising, because PMBOK Guide was one of the input documents for ISO 21500 and the development process for both documents was the same, i.e. a compilation of globally used good practices of project management;
- 90% of the process names are the same;

Subject area	ISO 21500 Process	PMBOK Guide-Fifth Edition Process
Integration	4.3.2 Develop project charter	4.1 Develop Project Charter
	4.3.3 Develop project plans	4.2 Develop Project Management Plan 5.1 Plan Scope Management 6.1 Plan Schedule Management 7.1 Plan Cost Management 9.1 Plan Human Resource Management 11.1 Plan Risk Management 13.2 Plan Stakeholder Management
	4.3.4 Direct project work	4.3 Direct and Manage Project Work
	4.3.5 Control project work	4.4 Monitor and Control Project Work
	4.3.6 Control changes	4.5 Perform Integrated Change control
	4.3.7 Close project phase or project	4.6 Close Project or Project Phase
	4.3.8 Collect lessons learned	-
Stakeholders	4.3.9 Identify stakeholders	13.1 Identify Stakeholders
	4.3.10 Manage stakeholders	13.3 Manage Stakeholder Engagement 13.4 Control Stakeholder Engagement
Scope	4.3.11 Define Scope	5.2 Collect Requirements 5.3 Define scope
	4.3.12 Create work breakdown structure	5.4 Create WBS
	4.3.13 Define activities	6.2 Define Activities
	4.3.14 Control scope	5.5 Validate Scope 5.6 Control scope
Resources	4.3.15 Establish project team	9.2 Acquire Project Team
	4.3.16 Estimate resources	6.4 Estimate Activity Resources
	4.3.17 Define project organization	9.1 Plan Human Resource Management
	4.3.18 Develop project team	9.3 Develop Project Team
	4.3.19 Control resources	-
	4.3.20 Manage project team	9.4 Manage Project Team
Time	4.3.21 Sequence activities	6.3 Sequence Activities
	4.3.22 Estimate activity durations	6.5 Estimate Activity Durations
	4.3.23 Develop Schedule	6.6 Develop Schedule
	4.3.24 Control schedule	6.7 Control Schedule
Cost	4.3.25 Estimate costs	7.2 Estimate Costs
	4.3.26 Develop budget	7.3 Determine Budget
	4.3.27 Control costs	7.4 Control Costs
Risk	4.3.28 Identify risks	11.2 Identify Risks
	4.3.29 Assess risks	11.3 Perform Qualitative Risk Analysis 11.4 Perform Quantitative Risk Analysis
	4.3.30 Treat risks	11.5 Plan Risk Responses
	4.3.31 Control risks	11.6 Control Risks
Quality	4.3.32 Plan quality	8.1 Plan Quality Management
	4.3.33 Perform quality assurance	8.2 Perform Quality Assurance
	4.3.34 Perform quality control	8.3 Control Quality
Procurement	4.3.35 Plan procurements	12.1 Plan Procurement Management
	4.3.36 Select suppliers	12.2 Conduct Procurements
	4.3.37 Administer contracts	12.3 Control Procurements
Communication	4.3.38 Plan communications	10.1 Plan Communication Management
	4.3.39 Distribute information	10.2 Manage Communications
	4.3.40 Manage communications	10.3 Control Communications

Figure 7.1 ISO 21500 vs. PMBOK Guide-Fifth Edition

- Two ISO 21500 processes (4.3.8 Collect lessons learned and 4.3.19 Control resources) do not appear in PMBOK Guide, however their activities are part of other processes;

Other notable comments from the comparison are:
- The more accepted term 'executing' in PMBOK Guide is called 'implementing' in ISO 21500 because the latter is more universally translatable;
- ISO 21500 includes no specific plans per subject group; the Project plans (the Project plan and the Project management plan) include the Subsidiary plans if applicable, compared to PMBOK Guide which has a management plan (scope management plan, cost management plan, etc.) for every knowledge area;
- The ISO 21500 process 4.3.11 Define Scope includes the PMBOK Guide process 5.2 called Collect requirements;
- The ISO 21500 process 4.3.13 Define activities under Scope compares with the PMBOK Guide process 6.2 Define activities under Time; it seems to fit better under Scope;
- The ISO 21500 risk processes are in line with ISO 31000, those of PMBOK Guide are not;
- PMBOK Guide divides Assess risks into Qualitative and Quantitative risk analysis; more detailed but the same;
- The ISO 21500 process 4.3.35 Plan procurements develops a concrete plan per procurement item, while PMBOK Guide develops a high-level procurement strategy;
- In the ISO 21500 process 4.3.10 Manage stakeholders the emphasis is on control, not on directing as in the PMBOK Guide which then better fits under the process Execution in the PMBOK Guide. With a mature team you don't need to execute a lot. The team does the work (self-management), the project manager does the follow-up (control);

- In PMBOK Guide process 11.5 Plan risk responses occurs in Planning. Although the ISO 21500 process 4.3.30 Treat risk also contains planning on how to act when the risk materializes, the majority of the work lies in actually addressing the risk when it occurs (change requests, execution of corrective actions, etc.) and, therefore, fits better in Implementing;
- In the ISO 21500 process 4.3.40 Manage communications the emphasis is on control, not on directing as in PMBOK Guide under Execution;
- The PMBOK Guide process 12.4 Close procurements falls under ISO 21500 process 4.3.7 Close project phase or project.

7.2   Comparison with PRINCE2 2009 Edition

ISO 21500 has been mapped to the PRINCE2 2009 Edition project management method[19], the version issued by UK's Cabinet Office in 2009. The ISO 21500 processes have been compared with the PRINCE2 themes, processes and some special items (i.e. tailoring, product and role). As part of the comparison the activities of the PRINCE2 processes have been reviewed to determine matches with ISO 21500 processes. In figure 7.2 the high-level matches are shown.

The overall conclusion is that:
- ISO 21500 processes have a very good match with PRINCE2 processes and/or themes;
- The name of the processes/themes may differ, but when undertaking a match they (partly) cover the same activities;
- Only one ISO 21500 process (4.3.36 Select suppliers) is not covered by PRINCE2;
- Procurement is barely dealt with in PRINCE2;
- Some of the PRINCE2 themes (i.e. items starting with a number between 4 - 10, being the chapter number in the PRINCE2 document) match with the ISO 21500 subject groups.

Subject area	ISO 21500 Process		PRINCE2:2009 Theme (4-10) / Process (12-18) or Tailoring / Product / Role	
Integration	4.3.2	Develop project charter	4	Business Case
			5	Organization
			12	SU Starting Up a Project
			13	IP Initiating a Project
			14	DP Directing a Project
			15	CS Controlling a Stage
			16	SB Managing a Stage Boundary
	4.3.3	Develop project plans	5	Organization
			6	Quality
			7	Plans
			12	SU Starting Up a Project
			13	IP Initiating a Project
			16	SB Managing a Stage Boundary
	4.3.4	Direct project work	10	Progress
			14	DP Directing a Project
			15	CS Controlling a Stage
			16	SB Managing a Stage Boundary
			17	MP Managing Product Delivery
			18	CP Closing a Project (for a project)
	4.3.5	Control project work	6	Quality
			10	Progress
			15	CS Controlling a Stage
			16	SB Managing a Stage Boundary
			17	MP Managing Product Delivery
			18	CP Closing a Project (for a project)
	4.3.6	Control changes	9	Change
			15	CS Controlling a Stage
			16	SB Managing a Stage Boundary
	4.3.7	Close project phase or project	10	Progress
			14	DP Directing a Project
			15	CS Controlling a Stage
			16	SB Managing a Stage Boundary
			18	CP Closing a Project (for a project)
	4.3.8	Collect lessons learned	10	Progress
			12	SU Starting Up a Project
			15	CS Controlling a Stage
			A.14	Lessons log
Stakeholders	4.3.9	Identify stakeholders	5	Organization
	4.3.10	Manage stakeholders	5	Organization
Scope	4.3.11	Define Scope	6	Quality
	4.3.12	Create work breakdown structure	7	Plans
			13	IP Initiating a Project
			15	CS Controlling a Stage
			16	SB Managing a Stage Boundary
	4.3.13	Define activities	7	Plans
			13	IP Initiating a Project
			15	CS Controlling a Stage
			16	SB Managing a Stage Boundary
	4.3.14	Control scope	9	Change
			10	Progress
			15	CS Controlling a Stage
			16	SB Managing a Stage Boundary
Resources	4.3.15	Establish project team	7	Plans
			12	SU Starting Up a Project
	4.3.16	Estimate resources	7	Plans
			13	IP Initiating a Project
			15	CS Controlling a Stage
			16	SB Managing a Stage Boundary
	4.3.17	Define project organization	5	Organization
			6	Quality
			7	Plans
	4.3.18	Develop project team	5	Organization
			6	Quality

Subject area	ISO 21500 Process	PRINCE2:2009 Theme (4-10) / Process (12-18) or Tailoring / Product / Role	
Resources	4.3.19 Control resources	10	Progress
		15	CS Controlling a Stage
		16	SB Managing a Stage Boundary
	4.3.20 Manage project team	15	CS Controlling a Stage
		16	SB Managing a Stage Boundary
Time	4.3.21 Sequence activities	7	Plans
		13	IP Initiating a Project
		15	CS Controlling a Stage
		16	SB Managing a Stage Boundary
	4.3.22 Estimate activity durations	7	Plans
		13	IP Initiating a Project
		15	CS Controlling a Stage
		16	SB Managing a Stage Boundary
	4.3.23 Develop Schedule	7	Plans
		13	IP Initiating a Project
		15	CS Controlling a Stage
		16	SB Managing a Stage Boundary
	4.3.24 Control schedule	10	Progress
		15	CS Controlling a Stage
		16	SB Managing a Stage Boundary
Cost	4.3.25 Estimate costs	4	Business Case
		7	Plans
		13	IP Initiating a Project
		15	CS Controlling a Stage
		16	SB Managing a Stage Boundary
	4.3.26 Develop budget	7	Plans
		13	IP Initiating a Project
		15	CS Controlling a Stage
		16	SB Managing a Stage Boundary
	4.3.27 Control costs	10	Progress
		15	CS Controlling a Stage
		16	SB Managing a Stage Boundary
Risk	4.3.28 Identify risks	8	Risk
		15	CS Controlling a Stage
	4.3.29 Assess risks	7	Plans
		8	Risk
		15	CS Controlling a Stage
	4.3.30 Treat risks	8	Risk
		15	CS Controlling a Stage
	4.3.31 Control risks	8	Risk
		10	Progress
		15	CS Controlling a Stage
		16	SB Managing a Stage Boundary
Quality	4.3.32 Plan quality	6	Quality
		13	IP Initiating a Project
		15	CS Controlling a Stage
		16	SB Managing a Stage Boundary
	4.3.33 Perform quality assurance	6	Quality
	4.3.34 Perform quality control	6	Quality
		10	Progress
Procurement	4.3.35 Plan procurements	19.6.1.4 Plans	
	4.3.36 Select suppliers	-	
	4.3.37 Administer contracts	C.4	Senior supplier (partly)
Communication	4.3.38 Plan communications	7	Plans
		10	Progress
		13	IP Initiating a Project
	4.3.39 Distribute information	10	Progress
		15	CS Controlling a Stage
	4.3.40 Manage communications	10	Progress
		13	IP Initiating a Project

Figure 7.2 ISO 21500 vs. PRINCE2 2009 Edition

7.3   Comparison with ICB version 3

As seen in chapter 5, IPMA's ICB version 3.0 consists of
competence elements, grouped into three competence areas:
technical, behavioral and contextual competences. In ISO 21500
the competences of the project members are based on the ICB
version 3.0, and these are mentioned briefly.

In Figure 7.3 ISO 21500 has been mapped to ICB version 3.0,
where the ISO 21500 processes have been compared with the ICB
'possible process steps' that are listed with every competence. All
ICB competencies are shown in chapter 5 of this book.

The overall conclusion is that:
* All technical competences are covered in ISO 21500;
* Half of the behavioral competences are mentioned in
  ISO 21500;
* Most of the contextual competences are dealt with in
  ISO 21500 in relation to developing the project plans and
  more extensively in clause 3 (Concepts).

All 39 processes in ISO 21500 can broadly be linked to all
possible process steps as listed in the technical competences
('hard skills').

Only six out of 15 of the behavioral competences ('soft skills') are mentioned in two processes of ISO 21500 (process 4.3.18 Develop project team and process 4.3.20 Manage project team).

One ISO 21500 process (4.3.3 Develop project plans) deals with eight out of eleven contextual competences ('environmental knowledge') and 13 other ISO 21500 processes deal with only a single contextual competence. Three competences (Program orientation, Portfolio orientation and Project, Program & portfolio implementation) do not link with a ISO 21500 process, but they are dealt with in the concepts clause of ISO 21500.

	ISO 21500	ICB 3.0
Subject area	Process	Competence (with comparable process steps): - T=Technical, - B=Behavoural, - C=Contextual
Integration	4.3.2 Develop project charter	T 1. Project management success T 3. Project requirements and objectives T 19. Start-up C 5. Permanent Organisation (partly) C 6. Business (partly)
	4.3.3 Develop project plans	T 1. Project management success C 1. Project orientation C 5. Permanent Organisation (partly) C 6. Business (partly) C 7. Systems, products & technology (partly) C 8. Personnel management C 9. Health, security, safety & environment C 10. Finance C 11. Legal
	4.3.4 Direct project work	T 1. Project management success C 7. Systems, products & technology (partly)
	4.3.5 Control project work	T 1. Project management success C 7. Systems, products & technology (partly)
	4.3.6 Control changes	T 1. Project management success T 8. Problem resolution T 15. Changes T 16. Control & reports
	4.3.7 Close project phase or project	T 1. Project management success T 20. Close-out
Stakeholders	4.3.8 Collect lessons learned	T 1. Project management success T 20. Close-out
	4.3.9 Identify stakeholders	T 2. Interested parties C 11. Legal
Scope	4.3.10 Manage stakeholders	T 2. Interested parties
	4.3.11 Define Scope	T 3. Project requirements and objectives T 10. Scope & deliverables C 5. Permanent Organisation (partly)
	4.3.12 Create work breakdown structure	T 10. Scope & deliverables
	4.3.13 Define activities	T 10. Scope & deliverables
	4.3.14 Control scope	T 10. Scope & deliverables T 15. Changes T 16. Control & reports
Resources	4.3.15 Establish project team	T 6. Project organisation C 8. Personnel management
	4.3.16 Estimate resources	T 6. Project organisation T 12. Resources
	4.3.17 Define project organization	T 6. Project organisation T 9. Project structures C 11. Legal
	4.3.18 Develop project team	T 6. Project organisation B 1. Leadership B 2. Engagement & motivation B 8. Results orientation B 9. Efficiency B 10. Consultation B 12. Conflict & crisis C 8. Personnel management

	ISO 21500	ICB 3.0	
Resources	4.3.19 Control resources	T 6.	Project organisation
		T 12.	Resources
		T 15.	Changes
		T 16.	Control & reports
	4.3.20 Manage project team	T 6.	Project organisation
		T 7.	Teamwork
		B 1.	Leadership
		B 2.	Engagement & motivation
		B 8.	Results orientation
		B 9	Efficiency
		B 10.	Consultation
		B 12.	Conflict & crisis
		C 8.	Personnel management
Time	4.3.21 Sequence activities	T 11.	Time & project phases
	4.3.22 Estimate activity durations	T 11.	Time & project phases
	4.3.23 Develop Schedule	T 11.	Time & project phases
	4.3.24 Control schedule	T 11.	Time & project phases
		T 15.	Changes
		T 16.	Control & reports
Cost	4.3.25 Estimate costs	T 13.	Cost & finance
		C 10.	Finance
	4.3.26 Develop budget	T 13.	Cost & finance
		C 10.	Finance
	4.3.27 Control costs	T 13.	Cost & finance
		T 15.	Changes
		T 16.	Control & reports
		C 10.	Finance
Risk	4.3.28 Identify risks	T 4.	Risk & opportunity
	4.3.29 Assess risks	T 4.	Risk & opportunity
	4.3.30 Treat risks	T 4.	Risk & opportunity
	4.3.31 Control risks	T 4.	Risk & opportunity
Quality	4.3.32 Plan quality	T 5.	Quality
	4.3.33 Perform quality assurance	T 5.	Quality
	4.3.34 Perform quality control	T 5.	Quality
		T 15.	Changes
		T 16.	Control & reports
Procurement	4.3.35 Plan procurements	T 14.	Procurement & contract
	4.3.36 Select suppliers	T 14.	Procurement & contract
		C 11	Legal
	4.3.37 Administer contracts	T 14.	Procurement & contract
		T 16.	Control & reports
Communication	4.3.38 Plan communications	T 17.	Information & documentation
		T 18.	Communication
	4.3.39 Distribute information	T 16.	Control & reports
		T 17.	Information & documentation
		T 18.	Communication
	4.3.40 Manage communications	T 17.	Information & documentation
		T 18.	Communication

Figure 7.3 ISO 21500 vs. ICB version 3.0

7.4   Comparison with Agile project management

Although ISO 21500 doesn't explicitly refer to iterative development methods, it also doesn't state that the project life cycle should typically adopt the 'waterfall' development approach. Given the huge overlap of ISO 21500 with the PMBOK Guide processes, the comparison between Agile and PMBOK Guide may be used as a valid reference for the comparison between Agile and ISO 21500.

Agile project management is based on the following principles: embrace change, focus on customer value, deliver part of the required functionality incrementally, collaborate, reflect and learn continuously. Applying these principles results in:

* Only plan what you realistically expect to happen, with a level of detail which is appropriate to the planning horizon (relatively short – the Agile manifesto talks of a two to four weeks cycle and delivery at the end of each iteration);
* Don't go for delivery of the project objective (Scope with a defined quality) in one go, but plan for several iterations instead;
* 'Control' is through inspection and adaptation using reviews and retrospectives by a self organizing team;
* This approach allows higher flexibility in Scope (embrace change!).

Agile practices which are used to manage change are:

* Continuous feedback loops;
* Iterative and incremental development;
* Prioritized backlogs.

The result is that Agile project management methods cannot be considered completely, from the traditional project management point of view, since a number of processes are either missing or not described explicitly. But then again, because of the reduced level of complexity there is less need to perform the planning and controlling processes to that level of detail.

Nevertheless, a detailed Scope is still defined (What 'features' are in the scope of this iteration?) for which the processes in the Scope subject group can be applied and a Schedule needs to be created, though only a detailed plan as we only plan to a certain planning horizon, for which we can use the processes from the Time subject group and the Budget per iteration (limited) needs to be planned based on the Resources planned for the iteration. Given the above, Agile project management is more of a method (how) than a project management guideline (what). In this respect, Agile and ISO 21500 are complementary.

One could even consider that through the application of program management as an overarching layer for a group of projects, Agile principles are introduced as well; instead of one big project, a well balanced set of smaller projects is delivered, maybe sequentially or in parallel, with each sub-project delivering benefits (and thus customer value).

Finally one should also respect that the Agile project management method is not suitable for every project. Imagine using an Agile approach for realizing a project with the objective of 'switching all traffic from left hand driving to right hand driving' as follows:
- Lorries, busses and trucks change in week one;
- Passenger cars in week two;
- All the remaining traffic (cyclists, motorists, etc.) in the third week ....

Subject area	ISO 21500	PRiSM V2.1 (2009-2012)	
	Process	Process / Activity per phase:	
		- 1 Pre-Project / Initiation	
		- 2 Project Planning	
		- 3 Executing and Controlling the	
		Project	
		- 4 Closing the Project	
Integration	4.3.2 Develop project charter	1.6.	Draft project charter/business case
		1.12.	Finalize project charter/business case
	4.3.3 Develop project plans	1.4.	Review lessons previous learned from portfolio manager
		2.1	Review project charter/business case
		2.3	Begin in-depth planning
		2.6	Refine sustainability management plan (partly)
		2.13	Finalize project plan
		3.2	Establish stage milestones
		3.3	Issue stage plan and work packages
		3.6	Update documentation
		3.10	Update project plan
	4.3.4 Direct project work	-	
	4.3.5 Control project work	2.5	Setup project controls and measurements
		3.9	Enforce change control process
		4.1	Review final milestones
	4.3.6 Control changes	3.9	Enforce change control process
	4.3.7 Close project phase or project	4.2	Review and close risk and issue register
		4.3	Plan project closure
		4.4	Prepare project handover to client
		4.5	Formal handover
		4.6	Carry out closing activities
		4.8	Produce end of project report
		4.11	Request formal closure
		4.12	Release project team
	4.3.8 Collect lessons learned	4.10	Distribute lessons learned to PMO (partly)
Stakeholders	4.3.9 Identify stakeholders	1.1	Select project sponsor (partly)
	4.3.10 Manage stakeholders	-	
Scope	4.3.11 Define Scope	3.1	Requirements management
	4.3.12 Create work breakdown structure	2.7	Create products breakdown structure
		2.8	Create work breakdown structure
	4.3.13 Define activities	2.9	Estimate work activities
		3.3	Issue stage plan and work packages
	4.3.14 Control scope	3.1	Requirements management
		3.4	Work package review
		3.5	Work package acceptance
Resources	4.3.15 Establish project team	1.2	Select project manager
		1.3	Formulate project team
		2.2	Create project team
	4.3.16 Estimate resources	2.9	Estimate work activities
		2.12	Complete resource map
	4.3.17 Define project organization	2.12	Complete resource map
	4.3.18 Develop project team	-	
	4.3.19 Control resources	-	
	4.3.20 Manage project team	-	

	ISO 21500	PRiSM V2.1 (2009-2012)	
Time	4.3.21 Sequence activities	2.11	Create Gannt chart
	4.3.22 Estimate activity durations	2.11	Create Gannt chart
	4.3.23 Develop Schedule	2.11	Create Gannt chart
	4.3.24 Control schedule	-	
Cost	4.3.25 Estimate costs	1.11.	High level planning and cost analysis (partly)
	4.3.26 Develop budget	-	
	4.3.27 Control costs	-	
Risk	4.3.28 Identify risks	2.10 3.7	Analyze risk to activities Manage risks and issues
	4.3.29 Assess risks	2.10 3.7	Analyze risk to activities Manage risks and issues
	4.3.30 Treat risks	3.7	Manage risks and issues
	4.3.31 Control risks	3.8 4.2	Update risk and issue registers Review and close risk and issue register
Quality	4.3.32 Plan quality	2.4	Define sustainability quality components
	4.3.33 Perform quality assurance	-	
	4.3.34 Perform quality control	-	
Procurement	4.3.35 Plan procurements	-	
	4.3.36 Select suppliers	-	
	4.3.37 Administer contracts	-	
Communication	4.3.38 Plan communications	-	
	4.3.39 Distribute information	3.6 3.11 4.9 4.10	Update documentation Submit end stage report Submit report to stakeholders Distribute lessons learned to PMO
	4.3.40 Manage communications	-	

Figure 7.4 ISO 21500 vs. PriSM

7.5   Comparison with PRiSM

PRiSM™ (PRojects integrating Sustainable Methods)[20] is a
methodology for green project management, that was developed
between 2008 and 2011 by GPM (Green Project Management).
It integrates sustainability with well known project management
practices from PMI, (UK based Association for Project
Management) and IPMA, and knowledge from a number of ISO
standards: 21500!! (Project management), 14001 (Environmental
management), 26000 (Social responsibility), 50001 (Energy
management), and 9001 (Quality management). Green project
management focuses not only on the deliverables themselves but
also how they are created. The 'green' project manager places an

emphasis on P5: People, Planet, Profit, Product, and Process. He has to become an innovation agent as much as a team leader and process driver, considering what the long-term impacts are of the project deliverables during planning and creation, and focusing on sustainability before the delivery life cycle starts[17].

In figure 7.4 ISO 21500 has been mapped to the GPM PRiSM Flowchart V 2.1. The ISO 21500 processes have been compared with the PRiSM's processes/activities (per phase).

The overall conclusion is that:
- PRiSM has a number of processes/activities focusing on sustainability, while ISO 21500 does not specifically mention it. However sustainability is covered by ISO 21500 process 4.3.3 Develop project plans, where it is stated that the project management plan defines the procedures for the environment, amongst other subjects;
- PRiSM has special processes/activities to sign off next phases or stages, ISO 21500 does not;
- The PRiSM flowchart is weak on showing 'control' processes in the themes stakeholders, resources, time, cost, quality and communication, whilst procurement is not covered at all;
- While the GPM website states that the new GPM Reference Guide To Sustainability in Project Management covers '… key aspects of sustainability related International Standards, the new ISO 21500 Guidance on Project Management …', its published flowchart is not (yet) aligned sufficiently with ISO 21500.

7.6 Comparison with Critical Chain Project Management

Critical Chain Project Management (CCPM)[21] is a **method** of planning and managing projects that focuses primarily on the resources required to execute the project work. It was developed by Eliyahu M. Goldratt. A critical chain is used as an alternative to critical path analysis. The main features that distinguish the critical chain from the critical path are:

1 Taking into account resource dependencies and their availability.
2 The identification and insertion of three types of buffers:
   • Project buffer;
   • Feeding buffers;
   • Resource buffer
3 Reviewing project progress and health by monitoring the consumption rate of the buffers rather than individual task performance to schedule.

In the CCPM planning approach the careful use of buffers prevents large amounts of safety time being added to all tasks within a project. By doing so, typical bad planning behavior like multitasking, student syndrome, Parkinson's Law and poorly synchronized integration are avoided[18].

ISO 21500 defines project management as the application of methods, tools, techniques and competences to a project, but does not mention any methods, such as Critical Chain Project Management. The project staff select particular methods to be used for the project at hand.

Related processes to Critical Chain Project Management in ISO 21500 are:

- The Resource-related processes 4.3.15 Establish project team and 4.3.19 Control resources, for which the resource availability is one of the key inputs;
- The Time-related processes 4.3.21 Sequence activities and 4.3.23 Develop schedule and Control schedule, where a schedule can be created and managed using the CPPM technique;
- The Risk-related processes 4.3.30 Treat risks and 4.3.31 Control Risks, where buffers can be assigned as a response to dealing with schedule risks and managed accordingly.

The Critical Chain Project Management method could be utilized in these processes as a technique.

7.7   Comparison with Event chain methodology

Event chain methodology is an uncertainty modeling and schedule network analysis **technique** that is focused on identifying and managing events and event chains that affect project schedules. Event chain methodology is the next advance beyond Critical Path Method and Critical Chain Project Management. Events can cause other events, which will create event chains. These event chains can significantly affect the course of the project[22].

ISO 21500 defines project management as the application of methods, tools, techniques and competences to a project, but does not mention any methods, tools and techniques, such as the Event chain methodology. The project staff select particular techniques to be used for the project at hand.

ISO 21500 deals with events in the planning processes 4.3.23
Develop schedule and 4.3.28 Identify risks and the Event chain
methodology could be utilized as a technique here.

7.8   Comparison with Process based management

Process based management is a holistic **management approach**
that guides the actions and mindset of an organization. Process
based management has a wider scope than the management of
individual processes. A process based organization explicitly
recognizes that it designs, manages and improves all processes
to optimize the delivery of customer value. Process based
organizations use this as a guiding philosophy and as a strategy to
differentiate themselves and outperform their competitors[23].

In essence, Process based management is a **method** to improve
organizational efficiency and effectiveness. To realize these
improvements quality standards, like ISO 9000, Lean and Six
Sigma are often adopted. It would be relatively easy for a process
based organization to adopt ISO 21500, being process based itself,
as a reference for managing its own projects and so increase the
chance that its projects are completed successfully. In that respect
Process based management and ISO 21500 are complementary.

7.9   Comparison with Lean project management

Lean project management is the comprehensive adoption of
other Lean concepts like Lean construction, Lean manufacturing
and Lean thinking into a project management context. Lean
project management has many ideas in common with other
Lean concepts; however, the main principle of Lean project
management is **delivering more value with less waste in a**

project context. Lean project management has many **techniques** that can be applied to projects and one of main techniques is standardization. Key techniques are those 'inherited' from Agile software development like: blame-free employee involvement, the need for a strong facilitator, pipelining, etc.'[24]

The five Lean principles are[25]:
- Specify value from the standpoint of the end customer;
- Identify all the steps in the value stream;
- Make the value-creating steps flow towards the customer;
- Let customers pull value from the next upstream activity;
- Pursue perfection.

Applying Lean to project management leads to the following Lean project management principles[26]:
- Eliminate waste;
- Instill empowerment, respect, integrity;
- Decide later, deliver fast;
- Amplify learning;
- See the whole;
- Manage risk.

ISO 21500 defines project management as the application of methods, tools, techniques and competences to a project, but does not mention any techniques, such as Lean. The project staff select particular techniques to be used for the project at hand. Using ISO 21500 as a reference for managing a project is not a guarantee for success, but it certainly increases the chance of the project becoming a success.

As Lean strives to deliver more value with less waste, combining Lean concepts and principles with project management would

lead to more successful projects. So when combining Lean with
ISO 21500 the chance for even more successful projects would
increase – projects run faster, have fewer deviations, deal with
less uncertainty and use less resources than without Lean.
In this respect, Lean project management and ISO 21500 are
complementary.

7.10 Comparison with Six Sigma

Six Sigma is a set of **tools** and strategies for process improvement.
Six Sigma seeks to improve the quality of process outputs by
identifying and removing the causes of defects (errors) and
minimizing variability in manufacturing and business processes.
It uses a set of quality management **methods**[27].

Six Sigma consists of three basic parts ('strategies'):

1 Process Investment;
2 Process Design/Redesign;
3 Process Management.

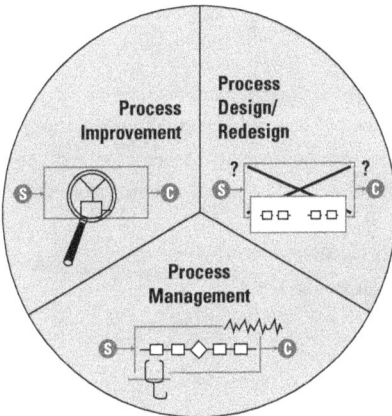

Figure 7.5 Six Sigma process improvement

'Process Improvement' tries to identify and eliminate the causes of undesired process outcomes or defects, produced by the process. The five steps of the 'Process Improvement'-strategy are (**DMAIC**):

1. **D**efine the problem and the customer's requirements;
2. **M**easure the defects and how the process operates;
3. **A**nalyze the data and discover the root causes of the defects;
4. **I**mprove the process by removing the causes of the defects;
5. **C**ontrol the process to ensure defects don't occur again.

'Process Design/Redesign' is applied when introducing a new product, or if one or more key processes are replaced instead of repaired or improved. In this strategy the steps are adapted to focus on the (re)design, and are as follows (**DMADV**):

1. **D**efine customer requirements and goals for the process/product/service;
2. **M**easure and match performance to customer requirements;
3. **A**nalyze and assess process/product/service design;
4. **D**esign and implement new processes/products/services;
5. **V**erify results and maintain performance.

'Process Management' is defined as a fundamental makeover in the way an organization is structured and managed. For this, 'Process Management' focuses on the entire process and not only on a specific defect or a redesign, with the steps as follows (**DMAC**):

1. **D**efine processes, key customer requirements and process 'owners';
2. **M**easure performance to customer requirements and key process indicators;
3. **A**nalyze data to enhance measures and refine the process management mechanisms;

4. Control performance through on-going monitoring of inputs/
   operations/outputs and responding quickly to problems and
   process variations.

ISO 21500 defines project management as the application of
methods, tools, techniques and competences to a project, but
does not mention any methods and techniques. The project staff
select particular methods and techniques to be used for the
project at hand.

When combining Six Sigma Process improvement with ISO 21500
project management practices, it is expected that the organization
will deliver more successful projects in terms of increased
customer satisfaction and less costs. In this respect, Six Sigma
and ISO 21500 are complementary.

Six Sigma, Lean and Process based management are in essence
all organizational improvement **methods**. Sometimes Lean and

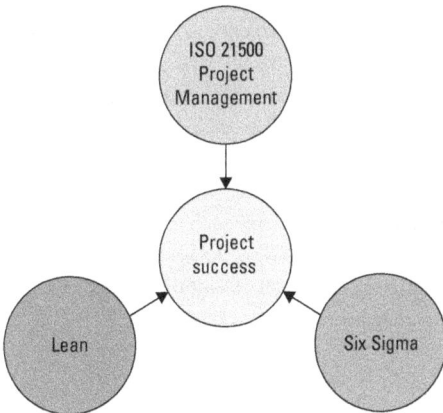

Figure 7.6 Lean and Six Sigma project management combined

Six Sigma are used together to optimize the performance in the organization and increase its success even more.

So combining both Six Sigma and Lean with ISO 21500 will increase the chance of project success.

7.11   Comparison with Benefits realization management

As a project focuses on the realization of the project objective, achieving the benefits (customer value) through proper application of the project deliverables is outside the scope of project management. It is the sponsor's responsibility to ensure the benefits are realized. Sometimes benefits realization becomes so complex that a separate role is needed to direct multiple projects in order to optimize the expected benefits and ensure that the benefits are realized when projects are delivered. This role can be fulfilled by a program manager. The program manager is of course working within, or closely with, the line organization or the sponsor entity that has accepted the deliverables to actually realize the benefits.

ISO 21500 refers to benefits realization (value creation) in the concepts, where in the organization based on the organizational strategy, opportunities (and threats) are defined, which subsequently lead to an approved project, via Business case approval in the project environment, through the application of project governance. The project delivers the project objective to the organization, which via its Operations ultimately realizes the benefits that were planned-for in the Business case.

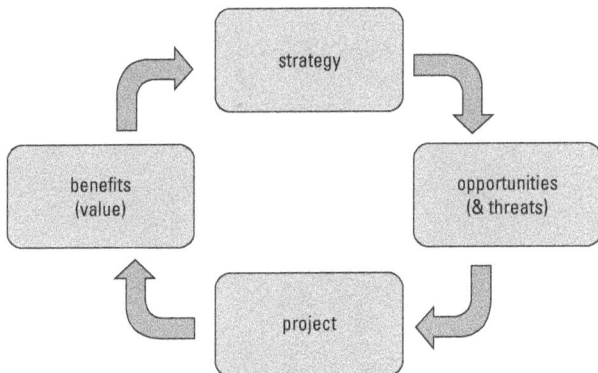

Figure 7.7 Value creation through projects

ISO 21500 describes this in the value creation framework
in section 3.4.1 Organizational Strategy, 3.4.2 Opportunity
identification and project initiation, and 3.4.3 Benefits realization.
During the project life cycle the project manager, when making
decisions, should consider the impact thereof on the planned
benefits and their opportunities for realization.

Note: The term 'organization' should be interpreted here in the
widest sense to cater for the differences in the environments in
which projects are executed. Refer also to figure 1.1 and the note
at the end of section 1.4.

8 ISO 21500 in practice

This chapter will provide a high level description of how the
ISO 21500 guideline can be applied in practice, using a rather
'generic' project life cycle as a reference, and explaining the
application of the different processes and their deliverables,
while going through the several project phases.

As a reference we will use a project life cycle as viewed from
the perspective of the project 'owner': this is the organization
or entity that is requiring and developing the project, whether
through internal resources or external providers, and
subsequently accepting the deliverables of the project.

8.1 The project life cycle – the key to start

To structure your approach for realizing the project, you will
first need to define your project life cycle: a defined set of phases,
from the start to the end of the project, executed in the order as
planned for. Each phase or sub-phase of a project life cycle allows
for the treatment of specific approaches, topics and techniques
separately, and based on the deliverables produced, provides
input to the other phases or sub-phases, and has a go/no go
decision point at the end. All project deliverables are planned for.
In order to allow a controlled progress and completion of each
phase or sub-phase, specific processes have also been described
to create the required project management deliverables (outputs)
for that sub-phase. This allows easy control and overview.

This project life cycle should be well understood by all
stakeholders of the project. In that way it will enable us to
effectively communicate the project's progress on time, based
on tangible deliverables. Phases enable a better control and

communication during the project. The end of a phase often coincides with the delivery of an end-product, a finished part of an end-product or a certain recognized status of an end-product. In most cases, authorization by a formal body (e.g. executives in a company or a steering committee) is required to start work on the next phase. A phased approach creates the opportunity to control, for example, investments during the project, or to have clear decision points within the project, thus supporting proper stakeholder engagement and communication at the right time.

According to the definition of a project, every project is a unique endeavor. Nevertheless there are some underlying generic professional best practices in approaching a problem and realizing the product, service or result. For example, in construction one can typically have the logical order of groundwork, foundations, building, finishing and commissioning. The uniqueness of the approach will be translated into the contents of the phases, being the (interim) deliverables, quality, specifications, etc. This all needs to be integrated into a project life cycle.

Some criteria for defining the quality of the project life cycle are:
- It is understood by all stakeholders;
- It is adapted to the needs of the organization;
- It has clear decision points that include a go/no go with clear decision criteria;
- It includes regular business alignment checks;
- It guarantees a smooth transition to operational mode;
- It supports adequate priority setting of the program or portfolio to which the project belongs.

Therefore, the project life cycle logically integrates the **project management deliverables** (or one could say the outputs of the project management processes) and the **product deliverables** (or the outputs of the product or service development processes). The number and content of the phases depends on the sector and/or the type of product and/or service to be delivered by the project. For example, one construction company will include 'foundations and ground and leveling work' in one phase while others will split it into two phases. It is obvious that the contents of the phases vary from the sector or product to be delivered: for instance, setting up a process plant is not the same as building an office.

Plenty of examples of project life cycles can be found on the internet, which can be used as a source of inspiration. These project life cycles can be based on practical experience (good practice), or may reflect an accepted or even prescribed approach in certain application areas (construction, IT, etc.), or for certain project types (services or solution delivery versus product delivery).

For our example, we will use a rather generic project life cycle. But in real life your project life cycle should be carefully aligned to different factors, for example, the project result, its application area and its environment, in order to properly reflect its complexity and to enable clear communication and gain stakeholder support. The project team should identify the most suitable project life cycle and adapt it to the project's needs, or perhaps even develop one for the specific project. Based on the fact that the project life cycle defines the foundational structure of the project, the project manager and the project management team, in conjunction with the project sponsor, should therefore carefully consider this.

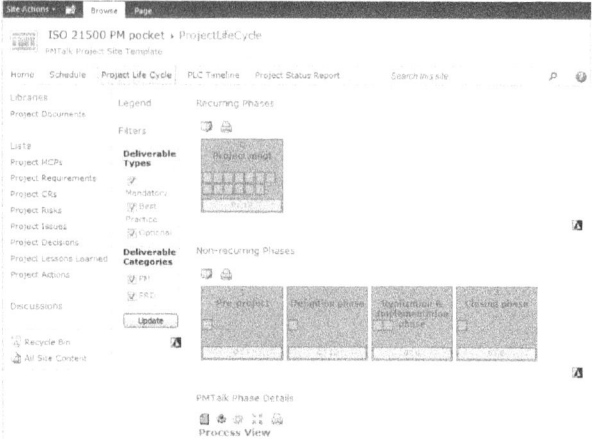

Figure 8.1 Generic ISO 21500 project life cycle

In our 'generic' project life cycle in figure 8.1 you will recognize
two 'layers':

- The **recurring** phases;
- The **non-recurring** phases.

The recurring phases typically contain the highly iterative and
therefore non-phase based project deliverables (mostly project
management deliverables), linked to the subject areas or themes,
like scope, time, stakeholder, etc. In addition to this, we also use
'Lists' for creating and maintaining iterative deliverables like the
Risk register or the Issues log. Of course one could position a
version of this deliverable in every project phase, but in practice
this appears to be too artificial.

The non-recurring phases reflect the actual phases of the project
life cycle: a logical time and deliverable based 'flow' from start to

end, containing all the deliverables which can clearly be linked to that phase. The 'generic' phases are:

1. Pre-project phase;
2. Definition phase;
3. Realization and implementation phase;
4. Closing phase.

8.2   The recurring project management phase

Your project needs to be organized in such a way that you are prepared to deal with all the different aspects proactively, without having the need to think "Now how should we deal with this?" In other words, be prepared, to:

- Create and update the project plan, at a minimum per phase, but interim updates may be needed to properly reflect the course of action as agreed by the project team, with all different aspects properly balanced;
- Effectively deal with issues and changes, as these will definitely occur during your project;
- Make and document decisions along the way, as you will have to take decisions but also should be able to track and trace these (who decided what and when);
- Address corrective actions, as the plan or the execution does not always deliver to expectations.

Deliverables which span the whole project life cycle and have a highly iterative character, are typically created in the recurring phase.

By consistently addressing all these iterative deliverables, based on the subject or theme which is covered by the respective deliverable, you will soon have gained some routine in your approach for the day-to-day management of the project at hand.

As deliverables in this section are highly iterative, several updates may be expected, based on progressive elaboration during the project. The deliverables which are clearly intended to be 'one-time' outputs should, of course, not be added here but assigned to the most appropriate phase.

Most iterative deliverables are typically updated at least once before the end of a non-recurring phase, thus creating all necessary output on all key aspects of the project as tangible input, before proceeding to the next phase.

⊟ **0.6. Quality**
  ⊞ Steps
  ⊟ Outputs
      ▭ Quality Plan (0) ▭
      ▭ *Attachments (0)*
⊟ **0.7. Resource**
  ⊞ Steps
  ⊟ Outputs
      ▭ Project Organization Chart (0) ▭
      ▭ *Attachments (0)*
      ▭ Resource Plan (0)   ▭
      ▭ *Attachments (0)*
      ▭ Resource Requirements (0)   ▭
      ▭ *Attachments (0)*
      ▭ Role Description (0)   ▭
      ▭ *Attachments (0)*
      ▭ Staff Assignment (0)   ▭
      ▭ *Attachments (0)*
      ▭ Staff Contract (0)   ▭
      ▭ *Attachments (0)*
⊟ **0.8. Communication**
  ⊞ Steps
  ⊟ Outputs
      ▭ Communication Plan (0) ▭
      ▭ *Attachments (0)*
⊟ **0.9. Risk**
  ⊞ Steps
  ⊟ Outputs
      ▭ Risk Prioritized (0) ▭
      ▭ *Attachments (0)*
      ▭ Risk Register (0)   ▭
      ▭ *Attachments (0)*
⊟ **0.10. Procurement**
  ⊞ Steps
  ⊟ Outputs
      ▭ Make-or-Buy Decision List (0) ▭
      ▭ *Attachments (0)*
      ▭ Preferred Suppliers List (0)   ▭
      ▭ *Attachments (0)*
      ▭ Procurement Plan (0)   ▭
      ▭ *Attachments (0)*
⊟ **0.11. Create (next phase) project plan**
  ⊞ Steps
  ⊟ Outputs
      ▭ Project Plan (0) ▭
      ▭ *Attachments (0)*
⊟ **0.12. Implement and Control project work**
  ⊞ Steps
  ⊟ Outputs
      ▭ Change Approved (0)   ▭
      ▭ *Attachments (0)*
      ▭ Change Register (0)   ▭
      ▭ *Attachments (0)*
      ▭ Change Request (0)   ▭
      ▭ *Attachments (0)*
      ▭ Contract or purchase Order (0)   ▭
      ▭ *Attachments (0)*
      ▭ Corrective Action (0)   ▭
      ▭ *Attachments (0)*
      ▭ Cost Actual (0)   ▭
      ▭ *Attachments (0)*
      ▭ Cost Forecast (0)   ▭
      ▭ *Attachments (0)*
      ▭ Deliverable Verified (0)   ▭

Figure 8.2 Overview of typical recurring phase deliverables

8.3   The Pre-project phase

We have an idea! The customer has a new demand! We have
recognized a new need! ..... Great.

Although all these triggers are a good starting-point for any
project, so far they are not projects.
The question is how to turn an idea into a formal project? Why
should we answer this demand? What do we need (deliverables)
to achieve this? How long can it take to prepare these
deliverables? What is the process? And who decides? Who is
responsible? Who pays for that? And so on.

These questions typically reflect what some application areas call
'the fuzzy front-end' of the project. In fact, our capabilities for
effectively dealing with this 'phase', which in reality cannot be
a phase of a project as the project does not exist yet, defines our
agility. It defines how quickly we can effectively respond to an
identified opportunity (based on an idea, demand, need, etc.), by
developing the Business case and eventually realizing the benefits
through applying the deliverables of a project. In an organization,
project opportunities can arise from anywhere. So having a
basic structured process for responding to them may reduce the
fuzziness or at least create a shared reference (guideline) for
effective cooperation in this phase.

Although all opportunities may be well intended, not all of them
can be realized (e.g. due to resource availability restrictions or
budget limits) and this should be accepted. There are current
priorities in an organization, defined by the organization's
strategy and tactics. New initiatives must support these priorities.
Given the priorities in an organization a persuasive Business case
must be built to assure the viability of the suggested opportunity
and to accept it as a project which fits into the portfolio(s)
and program(s) using appropriate project selection methods.
The Business case and the opportunity selection need to be
completed before any real project work can be started. Therefore
it is called a Pre-project phase.

ISO 21500 typically identifies two key project management deliverables in the Initiation process group that are important for the Pre-project phase:
- The Project charter;
- The Stakeholder register.

Project charter
Based on the approved Project charter the project's existence is formally recognized, including clear sponsorship of the project by the organization as well as the project's acceptance by the project manager. A high-level project description and key constraints like a certain deadline or budget limitations are included in the Project charter, as well as the Business case, explaining and supporting the reason for existence of the project. The key driver is how this project will be a means for realizing benefits.

Stakeholder register
Although it is part of the project initiation, in practice the Stakeholder register will be structured in the recurring phase. Firstly a high-level identification of stakeholders will enable us to proactively communicate to key stakeholders, maybe even involving them in the formal approval of the project start, thus creating their buy-in. But after project approval we need to perform a more detailed scan of the stakeholders, as they will have requirements which need to be collected for proper scope definition. As the project progresses, additional stakeholders may be identified.

Staff assignments and Staff contracts
As the key deliverable of the next phase, the project plans, needs to be created by the project team, we need to get at least some

key resources assigned to the project with requisite knowledge
of and experience with the key aspects of the project. This is the
reason why in the ISO 21500 process overview the Establish the
project team process, which creates Staff assignments and Staff
contracts, is placed under Initiation.

However, as the project team will likely need to evolve over time,
this is not a one-time effort but a recurring process. It is therefore
part of the recurring phase.

Project plans

Please note that in practice it is advisable, near the end of the
Pre-project phase, to also have the detailed project plan for the
Definition phase ready and approved. As the project plan is an
iterative and constantly updated document, this is also contained
in the recurring section.

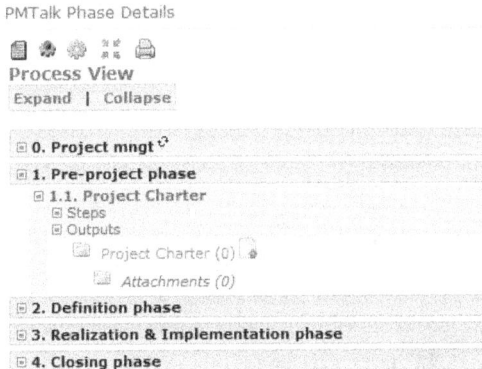

PMTalk Phase Details

Process View

Expand | Collapse

- 0. Project mngt
- 1. Pre-project phase
  - 1.1. Project Charter
    - Steps
    - Outputs
      - Project Charter (0)
        - Attachments (0)
- 2. Definition phase
- 3. Realization & Implementation phase
- 4. Closing phase

Figure 8.3 Overview of typical deliverables of the Pre-project phase

8.4   The Definition phase

We now have a project!

The Definition phase focuses on getting the project organized and describing how the project will deliver, which is translated into a tangible output called the **Project management plan**. This document or set of documents defines how the project is undertaken, monitored and controlled. The Project management plan may be applied to the entire project as a whole or to some part of the project through subsidiary plans, such as a risk management plan or quality management plan. Typically the Project management plan defines the roles, responsibilities, organization, and procedures for the management of risk, issues, change control, schedule, cost, communication, configuration management, quality, health, environment, safety and other subjects as needed. It defines the organizational set of references which every project team member will be using when delivering towards the achievement of the final project objective. In practice a section is created in the Project management plan, for all the subject groups (or themes) and for some recurring topics, which describes how the team will organize itself in order to deal with that subject proactively and consistently.

Take, for example, managing risks: How will we manage the project risks? What taxonomy do we use when talking about risks? What structure will we use? What risk-related data do we need to document and maintain? Where do we store the risk-related information? Who has what role in this respect? What tools do we use?, Etc. The same goes for a topic such as change management (what is a project change and how do we deal with these changes?) or issue management (what is an issue and how do we deal with that?).

As in the previous phase, before starting the Realization and implementation phase it is advisable to have the detailed project plan ready.

The **Project plan** contains baselines for carrying out the project or project phases, for example in terms of scope, quality, schedule, costs, resources, and risks. All parts of the Project plan should be consistent and fully integrated. The Project plan should include deliverables (outputs) of all relevant project planning processes and the actions necessary to define, integrate and coordinate all appropriate efforts for implementing, controlling, and closing the project. The Project plan content will vary depending on the application area and complexity of the project.

The Project management plan and Project plan are definitely not rocket science and once properly defined for one project a lot of the content may be reused for later projects. However, if this is not planned for and, as a consequence, not clearly communicated to the project team members and some key stakeholders, it will definitely lead to different interpretations and expectations. This is the root cause for a lot of misunderstandings, rework, loss of time and budget, conflicts, etc. with resultant adverse consequences for the overall project performance. Figure 8.4 provides an example of a structured overview of the project management deliverables typically produced during this phase.

The closing of this phase is the formal acceptance of its key deliverables: these comprise the Project management plan and the Project plan, accompanied by a brief Lessons learned document covering this phase. In addition, the first product deliverables may be created during this phase. The actual content is, of course, highly dependent upon the project's objective and

application area. As an example we insert the Product design
here. Then the next phase can start.

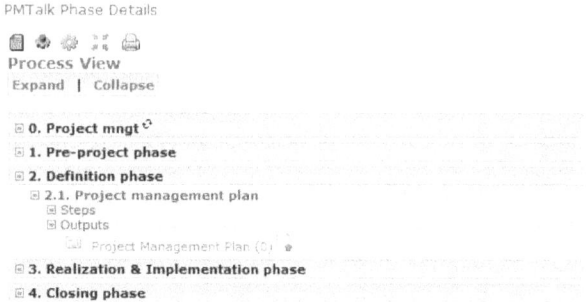

PMTalk Phase Details

Process View
Expand | Collapse

⊞ **0. Project mngt** ⟳
⊞ **1. Pre-project phase**
⊟ **2. Definition phase**
  ⊟ **2.1. Project management plan**
    ⊞ Steps
    ⊟ Outputs
        ⊡ Project Management Plan (0) ⭐
⊞ **3. Realization & Implementation phase**
⊞ **4. Closing phase**

Figure 8.4 Overview of typical deliverables of the Definition phase

8.5   The Realization and implementation phase

In this phase the majority of the deliverables are product
oriented.

Most project management deliverables are covered in the
recurring phase in section 8.2, as the focus is more upon refining
the already existing deliverables, due to the progressive nature of
the on-going work.

Lots of quality deliverables related to the product deliverables
may be expected in the Realization and implementation phase
as well. When quality control documentation is clearly related
to a product deliverable this may be stored in the appropriate
non-recurring phase. However when quality deliverables have
a more integrative nature these may be stored in the recurring
section 8.2.

This phase is typically finished when the end product is delivered, accepted and handed over to the sponsoring organization or entity, or to the customer. It may even contain post-delivery support to ensure a smooth transition. Nevertheless a clear cut-off point should be defined upfront to prevent continuous maintenance and support activities, which are of a more operational nature and could lead to a 'never-ending' project.

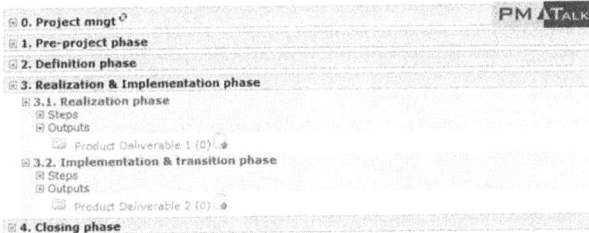

Figure 8.5 Overview of typical deliverables of the Realization and implementation phase

8.6 The Closing phase

This is the phase where the project is formally closed by a Project closure report. It provides confirmation that the criteria for customer acceptance have been met and requests sign-off by the project sponsor to close the project. In adition, all assets

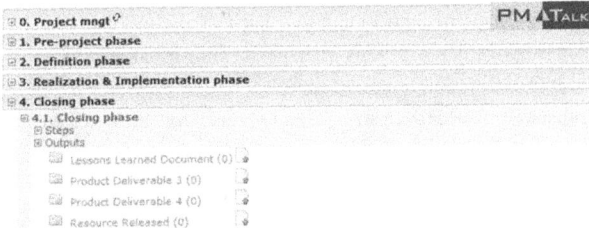

Figure 8.6 Overview of typical deliverables of the Closing phase

and remaining obligations, e.g. some procurement contracts with obligations extending over the project's lifespan (such as a guarantee), are transferred to the sponsoring organization or entity, or to the customer. This phase also typically contains the formal release of all resources, as well as a project evaluation document and Lessons learned.

8.7   Conclusion

The project management practices as reflected in ISO 21500, when properly prepared and structured upfront, can support a project team to make them 'ready for battle'. The exact structure and content of the phases needs to be well thought-out and appropriate for the project at hand. For larger projects this structure needs to be properly facilitated via a software application, which safeguards this well-defined structure, its consistency and proper integration of all the documents and data, to provide 'real-time' information on the project status and forecast.

For organizations doing the same types of projects again and again, having such predefined structures available for their different project types supports them in quickly growing their project management maturity. They will see considerable savings in time and cost, higher quality levels, less negative risks, etc. in their projects, which results in a better and perhaps even a leading competitive position. Using such a structured approach also supports organizations when performing a self-assessment on ISO 21500 compliance (see section 2.7), by providing a transparent and proven structured approach for the management of their projects.

Annex A ISO 21500 self-assessment

Here is an example of what a 'ISO 21500 self-assessment' might look like. See also section 2.7 for more background information on such an assessment.

Part 1 looks at the project management concepts and subject groups (themes), part 2 at the processes, as they appear in the ISO 21500 guideline. Part 3 is the undersigning, where the organization declares that it applies the concepts, subject groups (themes) and processes of ISO 21500:2012 to its project management practice.

By publishing it in the public domain, the organization shows that its project management practice conforms to ISO 21500.

ISO 21500 self-assessment		Question	Explanation	Source
Part 1 - ISO 21500 Concepts and Subject groups (note: numbering is as in ISO 21500:2012 document)		Is item relevant and used for projects?	If yes, explain how it is used	If yes, refer to relevant documents
3.2	Project			
3.3	Project management			
3.4	Organizational strategy and projects			
3.4.1	Organizational strategy			
3.4.2	Opportunity identification and project initiation			
3.4.3	Benefits realization			
3.5	Project environment			
3.5.2	Projects within organizational boundary			
3.5.2.1.	Project portfolio management			
3.5.2.2	Programme management			
3.6	Project governance			
3.7	Projects and operations			
3.8	Stakeholders and Project Organization			
3.9	Competencies of project personnel			
3.10	Project life cycle			
3.12	Relationship between concepts and processes			
3.11	Project constraints			
4.2.2.2	Integration			
4.2.2.3	Stakeholder			
4.2.2.4	Scope			
4.2.2.5	Resource			
4.2.2.6	Time			
4.2.2.7	Cost			
4.2.2.8	Risk			
4.2.2.9	Quality			
4.2.2.10	Procurement			
4.2.2.11	Communication			

Figure A.1 ISO 21500 self-assessment – part 1

ISO 21500 self-assessment	Question	Explanation	Source
Part 2 - ISO 21500 Processes (note: numbering is as in ISO 21500:2012 document)	Is item relevant and used for projects?	If yes, explain how it is used	If yes, refer to relevant documents
4.3.2 Develop project charter			
4.3.3 Develop project plans			
4.3.4 Direct project work			
4.3.5 Control project work			
4.3.6 Control changes			
4.3.7 Close project phase or project			
4.3.8 Collect lessons learned			
4.3.9 Identify stakeholders			
4.3.10 Manage stakeholders			
4.3.11 Define Scope			
4.3.12 Create work breakdown structure			
4.3.13 Define activities			
4.3.14 Control scope			
4.3.15 Establish project team			
4.3.16 Estimate resources			
4.3.17 Define project organization			
4.3.18 Develop project team			
4.3.19 Control resources			
4.3.20 Manage project team			
4.3.21 Sequence activities			
4.3.22 Estimate activity durations			
4.3.23 Develop Schedule			
4.3.24 Control schedule			
4.3.25 Estimate costs			
4.3.26 Develop budget			
4.3.27 Control costs			
4.3.28 Identify risks			
4.3.29 Assess risks			
4.3.30 Treat risks			
4.3.31 Control risks			
4.3.32 Plan quality			
4.3.33 Perform quality assurance			
4.3.34 Perform quality control			
4.3.35 Plan procurement			
4.3.36 Select suppliers			
4.3.37 Administer contracts			
4.3.38 Plan communications			
4.3.39 Distribute information			
4.3.40 Manage communication			

Figure A.2 ISO 21500 self-assessment – part 2

ISO 21500 self-assessment
Part 3 - Undersigning

Undersigned (name),
declares that (organization)   _____
                                                _____

applies ISO 21500:2012 Guidance on project
management for all its projects and
has assessed and reviewed this using the checklist
above.
The organisation declares that it applies the concepts
and processes of ISO 21500:2012 and guarantees
that this will be the case on a continuing basis.
This self-assessment will be assessed and reviewed
annually.

Date of assessment: _____
Name of the organization: _____
Address of the organization: _____

Signature: Location: Date:

_____

Figure A.2 ISO 21500 self-assessment – part 3

Annex B Glossary

The complete list of terms and definitions from Clause 2 of the
ISO 21500 document is shown below. It contains only those
specific terms that from a project management practice viewpoint
are not properly defined in the standard lists of ISO definitions or
in the Oxford English Dictionary.

2.1 activity
Identified component of work within a schedule that is required
to be undertaken to complete a project.

2.2 application area
Category of projects that generally have a common focus related
to a product, customer, or sector.

2.3 baseline
Reference basis for comparison against which project
performance is monitored and controlled.

2.4 change request
Documentation that defines a proposed alteration to the project.

2.5 configuration management
Application of procedures to control, correlate and maintain
documentation, specifications and physical attributes.

2.6 control
Comparison of actual performance with planned performance,
analyzing variances, and taking appropriate corrective and
preventive action as needed.

2.7 corrective action
Direction and activity for modifying the performance of work to bring performance in line with the plan.

2.8 critical path
Sequence of activities that determine the earliest possible completion date for the project or phase.

2.9 lag
Attribute applied to a logical relationship to delay the start or end of an activity.

2.10 lead
Attribute applied to a logical relationship to advance the start or end of an activity.

2.11 preventive action
Direction and activity for modifying the work, in order to avoid or reduce potential deviations in performance from the plan.

2.12 project life cycle
Defined set of phases from the start to the end of the project.

2.13 risk register
Record of identified risks, including results of analysis and planned responses.

2.14 stakeholder
Person, group or organization that has interests in, or can affect, be affected by, or perceive itself to be affected by, any aspect of the project.

2.15 tender

Document in the form of an offer or statement of bid to supply a product, service or result, usually in response to an invitation or request.

2.16 work breakdown structure dictionary

Document that describes each component in the work breakdown structure.

Annex C References

1 Project Management Institute, Inc. (PMI), What are PMI Certifications? http://www.pmi.org/Certification/What-are-PMI-Certifications.aspx, March 27, 2013

2 Society of Human Resources, Society of Human Resources Management (SHRM); SHRM – AARP Strategic Workforce Planning Publication date April 9, 2012 http://www.shrm.org/Research/SurveyFindings/Articles/Pages/StrategicWorkforcePlanning.aspx

3 Oxford English Dictionary, method, http://oxforddictionaries.com/definition/english/method?q=method, March 28, 2013

4 Oxford English Dictionary, methodology, http://oxforddictionaries.com/definition/english/methodology?q=methodology, March 28, 2013

5 Carboni, J., González, M. and Hodgkinson, J. (2013), The GPM® Guide to Sustainability In Project Management, GPM Global. Available at http://greenprojectmanagement.org/about-us/the-gpm-reference-guide-to-sustainability-in-project-management-ebook, March 28, 2013

6 Annual Report 2010 with summary of IFS Strategy 2011–2020. International Foundation for Science (IFS), 2011

7 BS ISO 21500:2012 Guidance on project management, BSI, November 30, 2012

8 ISO, ISO focus ISO 26000 Full issue.PDF, Volume 2, No. 3, ISSN 1729-8709, March 2011

9 Louise Bergenhenegouwen and Dick Hortensius, Praktijkgids – De 100 meest gestelde vragen – MVO volgens ISO 26000, NEN, 2010-2011

10 Guido Guertler, ISO 26000 an estimation, http://www.26k-estimation.com/, March 28, 2013

11 Oxford English Dictionary, role, http://oxforddictionaries. com/definition/english/role?q=role, March 28, 2013

12 Oxford English Dictionary, responsibility, http:// oxforddictionaries.com/definition/english/ responsibility?q=responsibility, March 28, 2013

13 Oxford English Dictionary, activity, http://oxforddictionaries. com/definition/english/activity?q=activity, March 28, 2013

14 Oxford English Dictionary, task, http://oxforddictionaries. com/definition/english/task?q=task, March 28, 2013

15 Oxford English Dictionary, constraint, http:// oxforddictionaries.com/definition/english/ constraint?q=constraint, March 28, 2013

16 Eliyahu Goldratt, Theory of Constraints, North River Pr; 1 edition December 1999

17 Oxford English Dictionary, competence, http:// oxforddictionaries.com/definition/english/competence, March 28, 2013

18 IPMA Competence Baseline 3.0, http://ipma.ch/resources/ ipma-publications/ipma-competence-baseline/, IPMA, March 28, 2013

19 Frank Turley (2010), An Introduction to PRINCE2®, http:// upload.wikimedia.org/wikipedia/commons/8/87/The_ PRINCE2_Process_Model_Book.pdf, February 14, 2013

20 Green Project Management (GPM), The PRiSM Project Delivery Method – What is PRiSM?, http:// greenprojectmanagement.org/prism, 28 March 2013

21 Wikipedia, Critical chain project management, http:// en.wikipedia.org/wiki/Critical_chain_project_management, March 28, 2013

22 Wikipedia, Event chain methodology, http://en.wikipedia.org/ wiki/Event_chain_methodology, March 28, 2013

23 Pat Dowdle, Starting the Journey Towards Process Based
   Management, http://www.bpminstitute.org/resources/articles/
   starting-journey-towards-process-based-management,
   March 28, 2013

24 Wikipedia, Lean project management, http://en.wikipedia.org/
   wiki/Lean_project_management, January 20, 2013

25 James Womack and Daniel Jones, Womack, James P. and
   Daniel T. Jones, Lean thinking. New York, NY: Free Press,
   a division of Simon and Schuster, Inc.

26 Lean Project Management Principles, by Hector Rodriguez,
   PMI Dade Dinner meeting, on Feb 19, 2010, http://
   www.slideshare.net/achiles6408/lean-project-management-
   principles-for-slide-share-3229562, March 28, 2013

27 Wikipedia, Six Sigma, http://en.wikipedia.org/wiki/Six_Sigma,
   March 28, 2013

About the authors

Anton Zandhuis, started his professional career in 1989 with the Netherlands Organization for Applied Scientific Research (TNO). He worked on large international research projects, focusing on the financial, business and project management aspects. He then moved to Arthur Andersen, managing ERP implementation projects and later Deloitte, becoming manager of the ICT project managers, implementing project, program and portfolio good practices as well as developing and implementing the ICT-Business alignment. In 2006 he joined Threon, a renowned European business partner for implementing excellence in project management, as Executive partner. Currently, as Head of Threon's PM Academy, Anton delivers project, program and portfolio management coaching, consultancy and training to organizations in several application areas (e.g. ICT, manufacturing, finance, R&D) for an international audience.

In addition to his continuous development in the project management profession, he was one of the co-founders of the PMI Netherlands Chapter (founded in 2000 – honorary member), served as Board member for several years in different roles, and became Board member of the Program Board Dutch Publications of the PMI Netherlands Chapter. He took part in the review team of the first Dutch translation of the PMBOK-Guide Third edition (published in 2006) and managed the Dutch translation of the PMBOK Guide-Fourth edition (published in May 2009). He was project manager and co-author of a Dutch publication explaining the practical application of the ISO 21500 guideline ('ISO 21500 in de praktijk', NEN, November 2012). He is a certified PMP as well as a Prince2 Practitioner.

Anton's drive is to share his passion and enthusiasm for the project management profession, as it's all about working together with people in innovative environments. He believes that, when applied pragmatically, it leads to motivated, more focused, and effective teams, which brings out the best of people, and ensures more successful project and program delivery and better and more sustainable business results as an outcome.

Anton is married, has two children and lives in Delft where he enjoys cooking with family and friends and riding his motorbike.

Rommert Stellingwerf, MSc in electrical engineering and PMI certified project manager (PMP).
Rommert started his career in 1977 with the oil and gas multinational Shell, where he worked for nearly thirty years in 14 different jobs, both in the Netherlands and abroad (Brunei, Philippines and Venezuela) for ten years. He has international experience in IT (from programmer to IT manager) and projects (varying from internal projects to large business startups and providing project consultancy and reviews).

In 2005 Rommert took early retirement and became self employed as owner-CEO of Staversk B.V. providing IT and project management consultancy. He has been busy since then as a consultant, as a volunteer and he is enjoying his hobbies.

From 2006 to 2012 he served as Director Education and Standards on the board of the PMI Netherlands Chapter. He is member of the Program Board Dutch Publications of the chapter, advising on Dutch (PMI) publications. He participated in the Dutch translation of PMI publications, such as the PMBOK

Guide-Third and Fourth Editions and the Lexicon of project, program and portfolio management.

From the early in 2007 he has been very active with the development of ISO standards for project, program and portfolio management. He is a member of the mirror committee for project, program and portfolio management with NEN, the Dutch standards organization. He is a founding member of the 'ISO for projects' interest group that reviews the practical use of developing standards for the Dutch market.

He was co-author of a Dutch publication explaining the practical application of the ISO 21500 guideline ('ISO 21500 in de praktijk', NEN, November 2012). Currently, he is convener of the ISO/TC 258 study group on project governance and a member of the working group on portfolio management.

Rommert is married, has two daughters and lives in Friesland, a province in the northern part of the Netherlands with lakes and canals, where he likes sailing in the summer, ice skating in the winter and maintaining his farm all year round. Other hobbies are bridge, playing and listening to music and travelling.

Van Haren
PUBLISHING

ISO/IEC 20000

ISO/IEC 20000 - An Introduction
Promoting awareness of the certification for organizations within the IT Service Management environment.

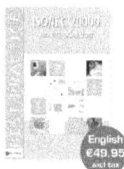

English
€49.95
excl tax

ISBN 978 90 8753 081 5 (english edition)

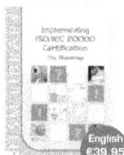

Implementing ISO/IEC 20000 Certification - The Roadmap
Practical advice, to assist readers through the requirements of the standard, the scoping, the project approach, the certification procedure and management of the certification.

English
€39.95
excl tax

ISBN 978 90 8753 082 2 (english edition)

ISO/IEC 20000:2011 - A Pocket Guide
A quick and accessible guide to the fundamental requirements for corporate certification.

English
€15.95
excl tax

ISBN 978 90 8753 726 5 (english edition)

www.vanharen.net

www.ingramcontent.com/pod-product-compliance
Lightning Source LLC
Chambersburg PA
CBHW032331210326
41518CB00041B/2062